Howard Cla

with contribution

and

GU00367181

Discovering
The Ridgeway

A Shire book

ACKNOWLEDGEMENTS

The route maps were drawn by Richard G. Holmes. They are not to scale. The Ridgeway path is shown by a heavy dot and dash line. The general map on pages 4-5 is by Robert Dizon.

The line drawing on page 6 is by Laura Potter. The photographs in the text are by Cadbury Lamb, as is the cover photograph. National Grid references are used by permission of the Controller of Her Majesty's Stationery Office.

A guide to accommodation, facilities and services, called *The Ridgeway National Trail Companion,* and a guide to public transport services are available from National Trails Office, Cultural Services, Holton, Oxford OX33 1QQ; telephone: 01865 810224.

British Library Cataloguing in Publication Data:
Clarke, Howard.
Discovering the Ridgeway - 7th ed.
1. Hiking - England - Ridge Way - Guidebooks
2. Ridge Way (England) - Guidebooks
I. Title II. Burden, Vera
796.5'1'09422
ISBN 0 7478 0534 2.

The Friends of the Ridgeway is an organisation committed to banning non-essential motor vehicles from using the Ridgeway, and returning it to a natural green lane wherever possible. It organises walks, tours and talks. The membership secretary is Mrs K. M. Crennell, Greytops, The Lane, Chilton, Didcot, Oxfordshire OX11 0SE. The website is at http://website.lineone.net/~friendsofridgeway/

Printed in Great Britain by CIT Printing Services Ltd, Press Buildings, Merlins Bridge, Haverfordwest, Pembrokeshire SA61 1XF.

Contents

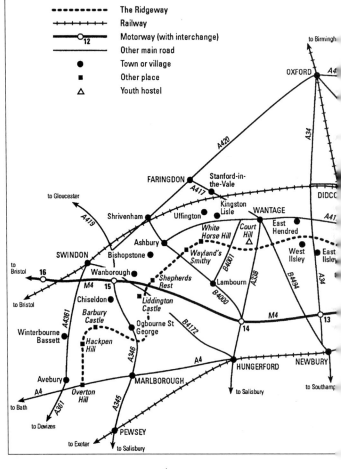

Diagrammatic map of the Ridgeway
(not to scale)

- - - - - - - - - - The Ridgeway
+++++++++ Railway
━━━O━━ Motorway (with interchange)
  12
───── Other main road
● Town or village
■ Other place
△ Youth hostel

to Birmingham

OXFORD

A4

A34

A420

FARINGDON Stanford-in-the-Vale

A417

DIDCO

to Gloucester

A419

Shrivenham Uffington Kingston Lisle WANTAGE

A41

White Horse Hill Court Hill △ East Hendred

Ashbury Wayland's Smithy West Ilsley East Ilsley

SWINDON Bishopstone ●

to Bristol

16

Wanborough ●

B4001

B4000

A338

B4494

A34

M4 15

Shepherds Rest

Lambourn

to Bristol

Chiseldon ●

Liddington Castle

M4

14

13

Barbury Castle ■

Ogbourne St George ●

B4172

Winterbourne Bassett ●

Hackpen Hill ■

A346

A361

A4

HUNGERFORD NEWBURY

Avebury ●

A4

Overton Hill ■

MARLBOROUGH

to Salisbury to Southampton

to Bath

A361

A345

to Devizes

PEWSEY ●

to Exeter to Salisbury

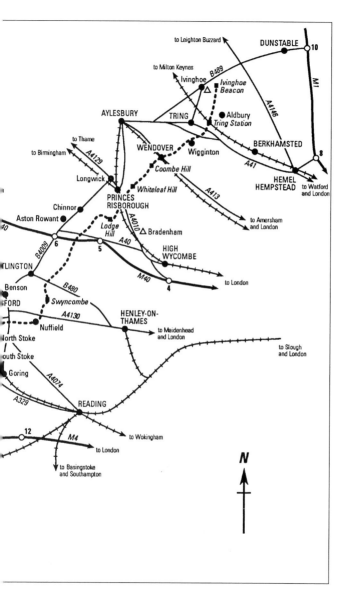

Pitstone post mill, near the eastern end of the Ridgway, is the oldest dated mill in England, believed to have been built in 1627.

1
Walking the Ridgeway: west to east
by Vera Burden

There is no better way of getting to know the Ridgeway well than to walk it. The long-distance path of eighty-five miles offers both a challenge and an invigorating experience. But although there is immense satisfaction to be gained from walking it all, there is no need to contemplate the entire length at one stretch. But however you choose to undertake the walk a little advance planning is worthwhile.

You can begin either from near Avebury in Wiltshire or from Ivinghoe in Buckinghamshire, allowing a period of several days in which to cover the full length of the path. This would necessitate either carrying camping equipment or leaving the path towards evening to seek accommodation in one of the neighbouring towns or villages. (Details of the accommodation guide are given on page 2.) Should you decide to look for accommodation, especially between Easter and September, it would be wise to make preliminary enquiries, as an overnight stop is not always easy to find. There are four Youth Hostels within easy reach of the Ridgeway: Court Hill Ridgeway Centre near Wantage, Streatley, Bradenham and Ivinghoe.

On the other hand, an exploration of the path may be undertaken in separate outings from your home base. By dividing the length into six sections averaging about fourteen miles each one can cover the entire Ridgeway path in six days although you may prefer to explore the prehistoric track in longer or shorter spells. The one problem of this plan is transport. Especially west of the Thames the region is not well served by public transport. Consequently the walker may need to rely on the amiable co-operation of a driver friend for setting down and picking up.

Whether you take Overton Hill, near Avebury, or Ivinghoe Beacon as the point of departure is a matter of personal choice. We walked from Overton to Ivinghoe, rather than the other way round, for two reasons: firstly because the prevailing wind and weather come from the west, and secondly because once over the Thames at Streatley, the path takes a decided northward turn, and so the sun is behind you. However, in this new expanded edition, the Ridgeway walk is described both ways. The walk from east to west is described in Chapter 2.

The first essential for an enjoyable walk is adequate footwear. No matter what season it is, strong shoes or boots are of primary importance if the outing is to be a comfortable one. Whatever the weather, it is always conceivable that you may encounter brief patches of mud here and there, and parts of the track, particularly west of the river, are heavily rutted. Also, as neither the barometer, nor the friendly forecasters of the BBC, nor red sky omens are infallible, it is sensible to carry some form of light waterproof and to be prepared in case a gusty wind is blowing, for it can be very cold on the exposed downland: the Ridgeway, abiding by its name, does keep close to the hilltops wherever possible. Early man travelled from one place to another by the safest route he was able to discover, so, rather than face a hazardous trek through the dense forests and marshes of the lower slopes, he trod out a path higher up. There, not only was it less wet under foot, but the traveller, by gaining a far less obstructed view, was reducing the dangers of his journey. The beauty of the path today is that it is well removed from the crowded roads, the busy towns and the noise and fumes of the traffic. The tracks our ancestors created from necessity have become for us a much welcomed form of relaxation.

There are parts of the Ridgeway where it is so wonderfully remote that there is sometimes no sign of a settlement for miles. But, except where the path passes through a small town such as Goring or Wendover, do not expect to discover places of refreshment on the way, though a short diversion will take you to one of the nearby villages or hamlets. However, you may well set off supplied with a flask and sandwiches, as once on the walk you will want to stay with it and feel no wish to break the continuity more often than could be helped.

From Overton to Streatley, that is approximately halfway, both horse-riders and cyclists are free to share the path with the pedestrian, but once across the river the forty or so miles of trackway from Goring to Ivinghoe are mostly confined to walkers only.

To assist the walker in keeping to the long-distance path various guiding signs have been placed at strategic points. These waymarks take different forms. The most obvious are the tall oak signposts saying 'Ridgeway Path'. Less conspicuous, and less frequent, are the low stone plinths bearing the single word 'Ridgeway'. This type is easily overlooked if you are not watching out for them. The third type is the small white acorn which is seen on posts and gates along the track and is the official waymark of all long-distance paths. The arrows next to it are colour-coded: yellow (footpath), blue (bridleway) and red (byway).

The waymarking as a whole is very good; some sections are almost over-endowed with waymarks, whereas elsewhere they are less liberally scattered. In describing the walk I shall make a special effort to supplement the official waymarks in these areas.

Nevertheless, the wise walker always carries a map, and if the way should be lost, the trail is soon recovered by looking out for the next landmark – the next hill, road or village. The 1:50,000 scale Ordnance Survey Landranger maps numbers 173, 174, 175 and 165 cover the whole trail. The 1;25000 scale Ordnance Survey Explorer maps numbers 157 and 170 cover the trail from Avebury to Wallingford bypass. Chiltern Society Footpath Maps 16, 15, 2, 10, 9, 14, 7, 3, 18 and 19 cover the trail from Goring to Ivinghoe Beacon at $2^1/_2$ inches to 1 mile.

The Ridgeway National Trail Companion lists accommodation and services and is available from local tourist information centres or the National Trails office (see page 2).

In addition, a pocket compass is of little weight and can prove very useful.

With all these essential preliminaries behind us, let us turn our attention to the walk itself.

The Ridgeway by Fyfield Down.

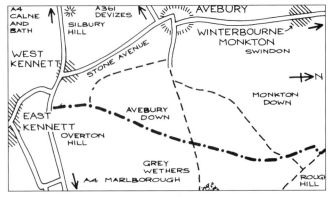

1 (eastwards). Overton Hill to Rough Hill.

Overton Hill to Wanborough Plain   16 miles

In Wiltshire the first signpost indicating the Ridgeway is four miles west of Marlborough, leading off the A4 at the top of Overton Hill. There is ample parking space here. On the south side of the road is a fence surrounding the ancient monument known as The Sanctuary; the wide Ridgeway path begins on the opposite side of the road, from the car park.

There are information panels by the start but the spot is sadly lacking in any landscaping appropriate to the start (and finish) of a major countryside attraction. The upland path is firm initially, but it is not long before it becomes rutted. Spurred on by low signs and occasional large stones which make good resting places, you are quickly rewarded by long views of rolling hills, often dotted with clumps of trees.

Possibly one of the first things of which you are aware as you step out is the exhilarating breeze. After two miles over the Avebury and Overton Downs, where the path is a highway between cultivated and pasture land, a sign off to the right indicates the national nature reserve of Fyfield Down. From here the path continues to Hackpen Hill.

The stile passed to your right should be ignored as the way proceeds ahead to pass a further nature reserve sign and then has a deep valley to the left. Soon gorse, that bright shrub which seems to flower at all times of the year, and thorn line the left-hand side, and the path is joined by one from Avebury.

A short distance on, the aspect changes to become less open and shaded by taller trees and bushes, and the path takes a right turn for a few yards to a signpost. Take care here. The track then swings left as indicated towards Barbury Castle and immediately curves right again,

10

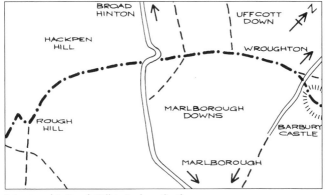

2 (eastwards). Rough Hill to Barbury Castle.

so that it has executed a short Z turn. Roughly speaking, it has now resumed its former direction. It has grown rougher under foot as well, and there is a possibility of some mud to be coped with as the path moves on, limited by wire fencing left and trees right. Before long it goes slightly downhill, where there is a connecting path to Winterbourne Bassett. The Ridgeway path carries on, uphill again now, to continue up and over Hackpen Hill. Although it is nearly 900 feet at its summit, the climb has been almost imperceptible.

On reaching a road – the first of those which intersect the route at various points, the path is quite clearly across it and forward. There are three fine groups of beech to be passed within the next three-quarters of a mile or so, all to the left, before the path is again

The path above Broad Hinton.

Near Ogbourne St George.

traversing treeless downland as it travels over the expanse of Uffcott Down.

Straightforwardly the path goes on to meet another road after a half mile or so.

A word of warning at this juncture may save you from missing the path. The original Ridgeway went up to Chiseldon: there is a signpost to this effect pointing along a forward left fork. But the *modern* long-distance path was switched to the more interesting route it is about to follow. So instead of walking on to Chiseldon, go forward and slightly right as signposted to Barbury Castle and Smeathe's Ridge. This leads you to a gate, which bears a request to shut it behind you. Naturally, this applies to all other gates along the path. More often than not the gates are there to allow us through and keep livestock in. If you are with a party please be especially vigilant in ensuring that the last person through does make sure the gate is closed afterwards.

Going straight up the hillside, the path is very quickly amidst the earthworks of Barbury Castle, which is cared for by English Heritage. This is one of the larger and more impressive of the numerous prehistoric earthworks punctuating the immediate vicinity of the Ridgeway. Here you are free to roam over the green arena. Then the path carries on ahead and, leaving Barbury behind, has wire fencing to the right. Nearly half a mile on it encounters another gate, with a polite reminder to close it as before.

This leisure area, Barbury Castle Country Park, with its commodious car park and toilets, provides a welcome excuse for a brief break, even if you are not in need of one; there is interesting information in the display shelter.

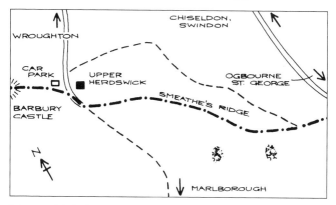

3 (eastwards). Barbury Castle to Coombe Down.

The path runs beside the car park and on for a few yards to the next signpost, pointing along a surfaced driveway in the direction of Smeathe's Ridge. This is Upper Herdswick, and the farm is seen on the left just before the path turns left through a gate. From then on the walk over Smeathe's Ridge is a joy. For quite a mile there is a ten foot ribbon of firm turf, delightful to walk on, and, as you stride along the ridge of the downland, there are extensive prospects of the neighbouring ridges and hills, particularly southwards towards Ogbourne Down. It is on sections like this that the exhilaration and freedom of walking the Ridgeway are experienced to the full.

On arrival at the next stile stay ahead; there is little likelihood of losing the way as the path is clear, but some 300 yards on, where it forks by a Ridgeway signpost, follow the left and lower fork to come down to a gate. Beyond it is a metal gate to go through prior to going forward again with a hill rising to the right.

The path is moving towards Ogbourne St George. Continuing its forward direction, two more gates are passed before a lane ushers you down to a road, where turn right as signposted to Ogbourne St Andrew. But 100 yards on, as the road bends left to Ogbourne St George, the Ridgeway keeps ahead along a lane. The waymarking is good here, and the shaded lane brings you after about half a mile to an obvious sign guiding left down a flinted track.

Now the path meets civilisation as it develops into a surfaced roadway, bridges the little river Og, curves between a decorative group of thatched houses and arrives at the A345. This is Southend, which, as its name implies, is just south of Ogbourne St George.

Cross here with care; on the other side of the road, travelling slowly

13

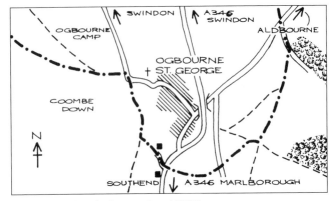

4 (eastwards). Coombe Down to Round Hill Down.

up a hedged lane, the path passes a disused railway line and crosses a further road. Once a sign has indicated that you should make a left turn, the ground becomes rutted.

It is about a mile on that a water tower makes a distinct landmark, just before the path goes left along a road, with Chase Woods right, to meet a crossing road, where it moves forward as a 'proper' path once more.

After another mile or so, where a side-path forks left down to Lower Upham Farm, the Ridgeway veers right for a pace or two before going forward again at the right-hand edge of fields to stay with the line of the ridge, journeying once more amidst the now familiar downland.

There is little likelihood of losing the path as it climbs the gradual slope of Liddington Hill and the tufted mounds which are the earthworks of Liddington Castle are seen not far to the left. Gazing down over Wanborough Plain, it is clear how strategic was the choice of such sites as Liddington Hill.

Returning to the present, the path bears right through a gate to cut between cultivated land before a gravelled track speeds down off the hills to the road at Wanborough Plain, which is the B4192. Being only two or three miles from the motorway junction at Swindon, and with parking possible in a nearby side-road, this suggests itself as a convenient pick-up point.

Wanborough Plain to Wantage   12 miles

At Wanborough Plain there is a temporary return to the present. The Ridgeway, as we have come to know it, has vanished, and a spell of road walking is unavoidable. The way is left along the verge of the

14

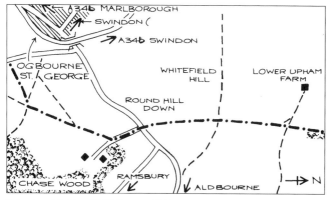

5 (eastwards). Round Hill Down to Upham.

main road for 200 yards as if towards Swindon. Then cross with appropriate care – this is a busy road – to walk right on the road to Little Hinton. This road crosses the M4 and takes you to Fox Hill, identified by the Shepherd's Rest public house. By walking forward over the crossroads by the inn you will soon discover the next Ridgeway sign on the right.

Climbing back up, the path is bounded by mixed hedgerows for several miles. En route it passes Ridgeway Farm cottages and traverses the invisible Wiltshire-Oxfordshire boundary. It is splendidly straightforward. Having covered about one and a half miles beyond the farm

6 (eastwards). Upham to Fox Hill.

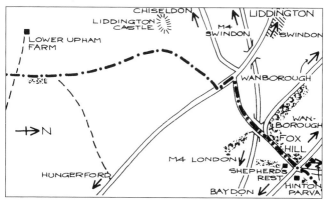

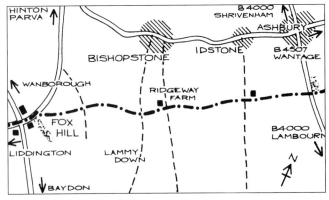

7 (eastwards). Fox Hill to Kingstone Coombes.

it encounters the B4000, just south-east of Ashbury, one of the most charming of all downland villages. Now you are clearly approaching Wayland's Smithy and White Horse Hill. For a while the path narrows to assume the proportions of a country lane.

The irregular stones of Wayland's Smithy attract hosts of visitors as well as the long-distance walkers of the Ridgeway. This is a popular spot, for the very next landmark is the earthworks of White Horse Hill; the path goes hard by it.

8 (eastwards). Kingstone Coombes to White Horse Hill.

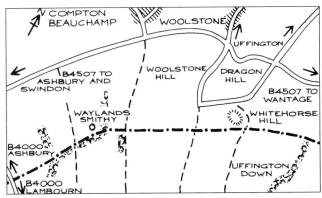

The Shepherd's Rest at Fox Hill.

From the top of the hill the path travels gently downwards and after a mile and a half reaches a road a little to the south of Kingston Lisle. Although no villages are included on the western half of the Ridgeway, there are several, including Compton Beauchamp, Letcombe Bassett and Blewbury, gathered along the foot of the downs.

Our path (distinctly heavy going hereabouts) switchbacks over two more downs to join firstly a farm track by a water tap on the right, then a minor road briefly, then crosses the B4001, one of the many roads to Lambourn.

Across the road the green track, ample enough to accommodate walkers, cyclists, riders and all, journeys south of the Devil's Punchbowl and Crowhole Bottom. On the other side the top of Green Down fills the horizon. Another mile and on the right is the striking group of ten beech trees known as Folly Clump. After a steady rise of about one more mile, at the top of Gramp's Hill the path crosses a narrow road going north to Letcombe Bassett.

Inclined to be muddy, the way pushes ahead, becoming less wide and densely hedged, for a quarter of a mile. As it broadens out, the downland vista returns. A farm is soon passed, and with Segsbury Camp off to the left, our path has developed into a mile of rough farm track, almost a lane, and firm under foot. This lane ends at the

Model aircraft enthusiasts on White Horse Hill.

Wantage road, A338, with Court Hill Ridgeway Centre youth hostel half a mile to the left.

Wantage to Goring   16 miles

An obvious signpost, by a house and a letterbox, marks the Ridgeway as it crosses the road, turns right for only 30 yards, then left as to Whitehouse Farm. Briefly the surrounding scenery is not the most exciting, for the land is arrayed with telegraph poles. But this is

9 (eastwards). White Horse Hill to Crowhole Bottom.

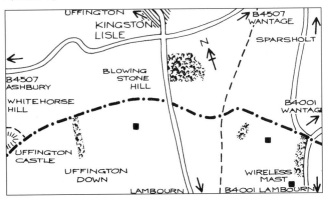

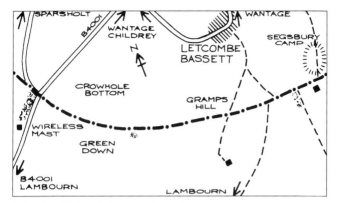

10 (eastwards). Crowhole Bottom to Segsbury Camp.

farming land, and there may be sheep and hens about. The farm road passes houses and a barn conversion. Beyond a collection of large barns and a farmhouse the road bends left and at a junction the Ridgeway goes right. Trimly hedged and deeply verged, a gravelled way, easy to walk on, twists between agricultural ground. Very soon it is replaced by the spacious downland track which corresponds to the preconceived image of the Ridgeway. It is well waymarked and, once you have taken the left fork when the way divides into two misleadingly similar broad tracks, it is straight on.

Having made its way over Lattin Down, the path crosses the B4494 and hastily bears right of a private road to a farm. Nearly half a mile

11 (eastwards). Segsbury Camp to Wantage monument.

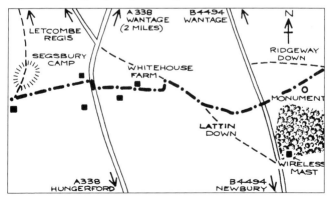

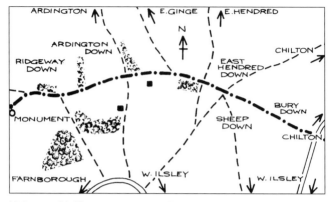

12 (eastwards). Wantage monument to Bury Down.

on stands the monument raised to the memory of Baron Wantage, soldier and farmer, who died in 1901. Away to the right are the fir plantations of The Warren, and the breadth of the Ridgeway surges ahead over Ridgeway Down.

At a copse and car park on Cuckhamsley Hill a rough road joins from the left. The trail continues straight on, although almost unnoticeably the Ridgeway has changed direction; it is now journeying south-east to pass between East Hendred and Sheep Down. There are inevitable glimpses of Harwell Research Establishment and the huge towers of the Didcot power station.

The minor road down to West Ilsley (car parking here) is crossed before the path strides Bury Down for another mile to the Newbury road (A34) at Gore Hill. At this junction the way is clearly under the road, and a signpost soon confirms the route. Just beyond it a modest stone on the left bears a touching tribute to a nineteen-year-old lieutenant in the Life Guards who lost his life in an armoured-car accident nearby.

The present long-distance path, continuing its south-easterly direction along Several Down, briefly diverges from the ancient Ridgeway, which was a little to the north. The chalk track carries on ahead to be replaced by a concrete drive on passing the Agricultural Research Station. On the right is a water tap by a stone carrying a plaque to a local doctor. When the drive soon meets a broad crossing track, stop going forward and turn sharp left, with a wooden fence left. The direction has altered to proceed east-north-east.

The uneven going is a trifle hard on the feet at first, but not for long. The signs are frequent and, after crossing over the little railway bridge (disused line), the path, worn deep into the chalk, is bordered by

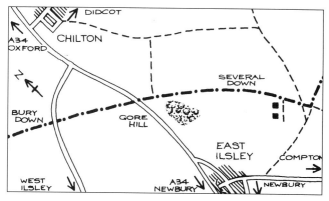

13 (eastwards). Bury Down to Blewbury Hill.

bushes. Walking on to Roden Downs, the site of a Roman temple is away to the left, and you will find that these paths are well used. This is one of the popular stretches. A lovely spot, Roden Downs is a veritable Clapham Junction of footpaths and one of the pleasantest places at which to rest awhile and take stock of the surrounding countryside.

About half a mile on, beyond Roden Downs, immediately after a crossing track the path forks slightly left, and before long curves past Warren Farm, Aldworth, where beware of mud! Then it becomes firm, soon to hasten downhill for about one mile to a second Warren Farm, below Thurle Down at Streatley.

14 (eastwards). Blewbury Hill to Warren Farm.

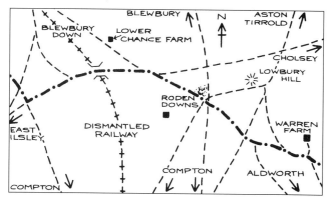

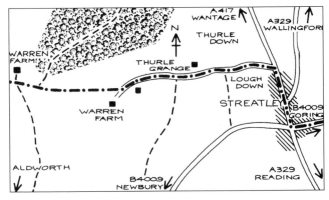

15 (eastwards). Warren Farm to Goring.

It is level walking now, for the path, departing from the downs, follows a country road quite peacefully, past a flourishing golf club, and below Lough Down for over a mile, before meeting the main road (A417). The direction is then right all the way to the traffic lights; then it is left over the bridge and a picturesque reach of the Thames, to leave Streatley and enter Goring and Oxfordshire. There is a youth hostel at Streatley.

Goring to Watlington   **14 miles**

Goring is a lively little place, having the holiday spirit common to many Thames-side towns. It shares a station with Streatley. From our immediate point of view it marks an important division in the Ridgeway. Between here and Ivinghoe Beacon walkers have much of the path to themselves.

To regain the path it is necessary to walk up Thames Road, situated between the bridge and the Miller of Mansfield. When the road bends right keep forward along a path to another road opposite Clevemede. Continue along this but maintain your northerly direction when it bends away, following a track that runs high above the river, parallel to the railway. On joining another road, marked private, keep forward past houses and presently the way becomes a path again, crossing a field to South Stoke, with its thatch and church over seven hundred years old.

Walk through the village and bear left down a lane to the river. Follow the towpath, passing under a railway bridge. Soon the path leaves the riverbank beneath some trees and shortly turns left and right to pass through several fields and gardens before entering the churchyard at North Stoke. (Dame Clara Butt is buried by the church.)

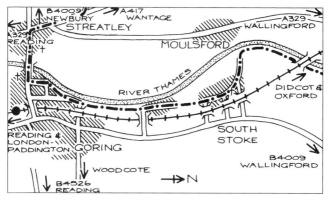

16 (eastwards). Goring to South Stoke.

Leaving the churchyard through the lychgate, go along the lane then left in this attractive village to continue northwards, crossing Mongewell Park and walking alongside a golf course to approach Carmel College. Keep forward along the metalled drive but once past the buildings leave it to proceed along a paved pathway to the left of a large field. Some 300 yards on by low brick piers turn sharply right

The Miller of Mansfield at Goring.

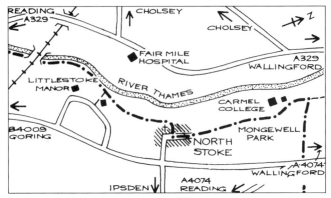

17 (eastwards). South Stoke to Mongewell Park.

along a belt of trees to march east alongside the Wallingford bypass and cross the Wallingford to Reading road (A4074). Continuing, to abide by the line of Grim's Ditch for the next three miles, the path reflects its truly prehistoric significance. It is a raised way, hedged by wayside trees and shrubs, thrusting determinedly on. When Grim's Ditch ends go left up a belt of trees and follow the edge of a field to meet the road at Nuffield. Then there is a turn right for a few yards only to a gate on the left. From here, leaving the village, the path travels diagonally right over a field and hastens on across the Huntercombe Golf Course marked by a series of white posts, through a wood in the course, and on to reach the Henley road (A4130), near

18 (eastwards). Mongewell Park to Nuffield.

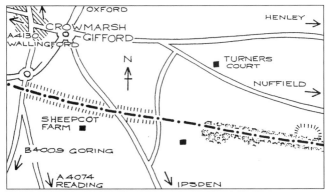

The parish church at North Stoke.

the Crown at Nuffield Common.

Journeying over the Chiltern Hills now, the path crosses the road to bear north-west, at first through woodland, then turns resolutely north to drop down into a valley. Turn left for a few yards inside a wood, then right to climb across a large field (aim for a white sign) and on to Ewelme Park, well south-east of Ewelme village. Pass the house on your left, into the farmyard, where turn right up a farm track to a field. Follow the right-hand field edge to woods and continue down a steep path to a pleasing valley. These pastoral scenes are one of the outstanding sections. Reaching a wide lane, where it swings right to pass the tiny isolated Norman church of Swyncombe, the path curves up, over a road, to wend its tranquil course upwards.

Cutting through woodland, it swings left to North Farm, slightly south of Britwell. At this stage the Ridgeway bears right to join the Icknield Way. Level, and at first of a goodly width, it pursues a steady north-easterly direction.

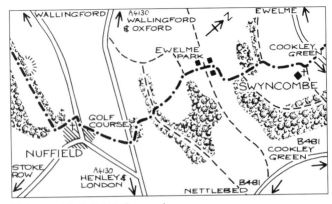

19 (eastwards). Nuffield to Swyncombe.

Were it not for the map, there is nothing to tell you this is the Icknield Way, but after about one mile, a little south of Watlington, there is, at a road, a letterbox marked 'Icknield'. This landmark is closely followed by a meeting with the B480 and then on to Hill Road, where, if one wishes to leave the Ridgeway, it is very easy to walk down the hill into the old market town of Watlington.

The Ridgeway Path leaving Nuffield for Nuffield Common.

The Norman church at Swyncombe.

Watlington to Wendover   16 miles

From Watlington Hill, cared for by the National Trust, the two ancient tracks move on as one for several miles. You can just stride happily along. Then, approximately three miles from Watlington, there is a sudden jolt back into modern times, when the path leads through a large tunnel under the M40. Proceeding, it quickly reaches the A40 near Aston Rowant. Having crossed the A40, the Ridgeway then reappears as a placid rural track forging forward.

On nearing Chinnor there is a diversion from the distant prospects

20 (eastwards). Swyncombe to Watlington.

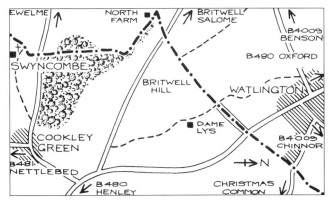

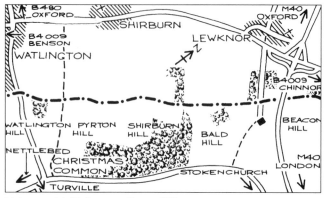

21 (eastwards). Watlington to Beacon Hill.

of the Oxfordshire plain. The quarrying of chalk has resulted in a lunar landscape to either side of the path.

After skirting Chinnor the long-distance path branches off from the Icknield Way, which exists as a metalled road through much of Buckinghamshire. Turning eastwards by a house at a junction of paths at Hempton Wainhill, it traverses the county boundary into Buckinghamshire. Much narrower here, it climbs up into woodland. On emerging at a crosstrack the way is ahead for a few yards, but then right through a gate hidden in the hedge. Entering a large field, cut across the corner leftwards to pick up a left-hand hedge and follow this towards the far corner, where a gate gives entry to another field. Turn

22 (eastwards). Beacon Hill to Chinnor.

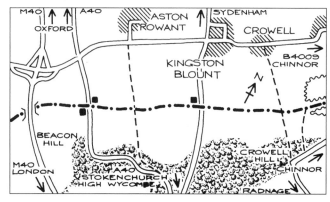

From Wigans Lane, south of Princes Risborough, towards Lodge Hill.

right by the hedge, cross a road, and the path clambers up Lodge Hill to give scenic views on every side. Anywhere between here and Whiteleaf Hill is convenient for branching off to the small youth hostel at Bradenham.

Looping to turn north, the path descends through a field and crosses a road, passes through a field and a gate and crosses a golf course to a couple of railway lines, the first unguarded, the second over the end of a tunnel, and crossing a field under power lines emerges on a road, where it turns right. After a stretch of country road walking for a

23 (eastwards). Chinnor to Lodge Hill.

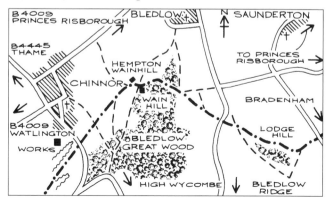

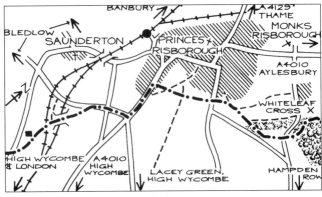

24 (eastwards). Lodge Hill to Whiteleaf Cross.

quarter of a mile to the A4010, the direction turns north for another quarter-mile. Being prone to heavy traffic, this short stretch is the least prepossessing of the entire route. But it is not for long, and just prior to Princes Risborough the road is abandoned and a sign guides along a broad track on the right.

The Ridgeway is briefly reunited with the Icknield Way. Making a steady incline, our path crosses a road, then soon bears right uphill, following the right-hand side of two fields, then climbing steeply through scrub to a gate into a field near the hilltop. Maintain your direction to a stile leading on to a road but do not climb it; instead bear left, between hawthorns, and pass beneath trees into the corner.

25 (eastwards). Whiteleaf Cross to Coombe Hill.

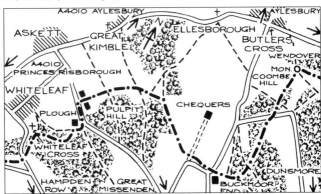

Continue through a nature reserve to a road. At the far side is a large picnic and parking place. It would be an admirable prearranged meeting place if a friend had agreed to join you part-way.

At this point the path is forward between the trees. On coming out into the open by a barrow, just above Whiteleaf Cross, which was cut into the chalk in the distant past, turn right to pick up a path wending its way through a beechwood of exceptional beauty, carpeted by layer upon layer of russet leaf and down a steep slope.

The Plough at Lower Cadsden is the next landmark. Occupying an ideal position at the end of a long valley, this is one of the few inns located directly on the Ridgeway.

When ready to go on, walk away from the inn, past the cottages, to the road. Turn left until a signpost indicates the way through a gate on the right. The path climbs steeply (steps make it easier), then emerges into the open, crossing a field along a ridge, to enter a nature reserve. Shortly after crossing a bridlepath, a waymarked gate will be reached.

The monument on Coombe Hill, near Wendover.

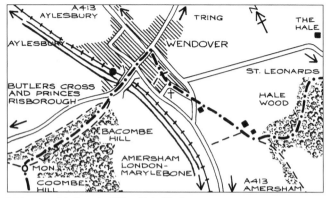

26 (eastwards). Coombe Hill to Hale Wood.

Pass through it and turn up the tussocky grass of the hillside. As the path wanders on by way of two more gates, it moves right to loop round the deep coomb known as Happy Valley.

Then, still inclining right, the path cuts across a field to go round the Chequers estate, which was given to the country by Lord Lee of Fareham as a country home for the prime minister of the day. Cross the Chequers drive and keep on to a road. Take the tree-lined track opposite leading into a wood; go over a crossing path and continue uphill, but soon veer left on a clearly waymarked path through the beeches to a road. A few yards to the right turn left into woods, keeping near their right-hand edge until reaching open ground on the left. Now follow the line of bushes on the shoulder of the ridge to the monument at the top of Coombe Hill, generally accepted as the highest summit of the Chilterns. You will want to stop and look about, for there are spreading views, across Wendover to the escarpment of Boddington Hill, noted for its beech hangings, and north over the Vale of Aylesbury.

From the monument crowning the top, a sign directs you on (the path is the less clear of the two leading away to the right from the monument) and down Bacombe Hill, through an area of scrub down to the Ellesborough Road, where turn right down into Wendover.

Wendover to Ivinghoe Beacon 11 miles

Whereas the path was able to follow the line of the escarpment and avoid the town of Watlington altogether, in Wendover this has not been possible. From the foot of Bacombe Hill it journeys straight down the main street, which is the Icknield Way, aiming at the Clock Tower at the bottom. Immediately short of it, and just beyond the Red Lion, the

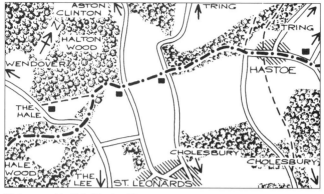

27 (eastwards). Hale Wood to Hastoe.

Ridgeway goes right on a well-used pathway. Keeping cheerful pace with a sparkling stream, it is an attractive path, though far more civilised than the remoter tracks to which we have grown accustomed. It is the link between town and church, where our way is left along the rural road, soon to cross another minor road at Wellhead.

A deeply sunken chalk track takes over, and beyond Boswells farm it speedily goes left to wander amidst Forestry Commission ground. Ascending steadily, as it has been doing ever since Wellhead, the path

Wendover's parish church.

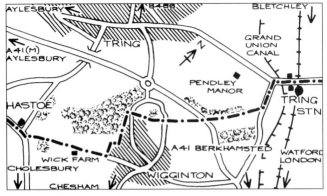

28 (eastwards). Hastoe to Tring station.

wanders left towards the top, to be trodden out along the line of the hill. In the winter there are more panoramic views of the Vale here, with Wendover in the foreground.

The next landmark is the road by Uphill Farm, from whence the path heads for the sylvan splendour of Wendover Woods. Rapidly dipping down, it provides an endearing glimpse of Hale Farm framed by the branches to the left. This lap is marked for its constant series of ups and downs, and it is advisable to allow plenty of time for these last undulating miles. The path turns sharply right, uphill along a sunken track, until, near Chivery, it meets a double signpost, that is, pointing forward and back. Go over a road into meadowland to gain the next road behind farm buildings at the far left corner but only a few paces of road here, for the Ridgeway enters a wood. Staying near the wood's right boundary and crossing a clearing, it emerges on a road.

Keep left along the road to a fork at Hastoe, where take the right-hand road. At a T junction keep straight on to a gate and follow the track past Wick Farm and on towards Wigginton. Just before a bungalow on the left turn left over a stile and follow the edge of a field, adjacent to gardens. After the last garden turn right, following the hedge of an area of rough grass. The path runs between bushes and beneath two cedars to a corner. Turn left, keeping the hedge on your right, and at a telegraph pole keep straight on, crossing the drive of Rangers Cottage, at the edge of woodland to a gate. Turn right to a road, where a gate opposite marks the way, mostly between fencing, to another road. Go right for a few paces and enter a field on the left, then follow its left side to a gate in the corner. Continue downhill to meet and cross by a high footbridge the A41 Tring bypass and onwards after a short distance to cross with care the old Tring to Watford road. Turn

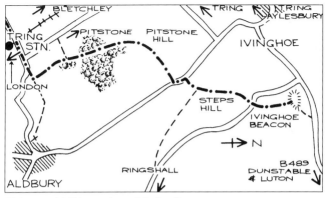

29 (eastwards). Tring station to Ivinghoe Beacon.

right to a house, from where the path skirts the grounds of Pendley Manor Hotel through fields to join a road. This is an interesting stretch of road walking. First, it crosses the canal, and Tring was the highest point on the route of the London to Birmingham canal system. Then, it passes Tring station, which is a couple of miles from the town. Beyond the station, soon after a road junction, the path forks left up a concreted drive and on to a crosspath. Go left along this, to head for the woodland of Aldbury Nowers.

The walk is nearly over. It will end, as it began, on the breezy heights of the chalk downs. Climbing over Pitstone Hill, the Beacon, a noble spur of the Chilterns, hoves into view. Down there at Pitstone Green is one of the oldest windmills in England.

Picnic tables below Pitstone Hill.

Crossing a road, the path treks on and up to swing left and follow the top of the ridge. It ventures down to cross a final road before a sign guides walkers on to the summit of Ivinghoe Beacon, the end of the Ridgeway.

Although the Ridgeway path ends here, the ancient Icknield Way continued along the Chilterns into Norfolk. *The Icknield Way Path: A Walkers' Guide* is available from the Icknield Way Association, 19 Boundary Road, Bishop's Stortford, Hertfordshire CM23 5LE (telephone: 01279 504602) or good bookshops. A leaflet on the 'Two Ridges Link', linking the Beacon and the Greensand Ridge Walk, is available from Buckinghamshire County Council, Shire Hall, Aylesbury (telephone: 01296 382171).

2
Walking the Ridgeway: east to west
by Howard Clarke

The Ridgeway starts by the trig point at the top of Ivinghoe Beacon. For those being dropped off by car there is a small car park on the B489 (grid reference SP 963172) below the Beacon opposite the junction with a minor road to Ivinghoe Aston. A steep path leads upwards from the right-hand corner of the car park to a stile on the left. Ignore this and turn right here to the summit and the start.

Rail travellers will find Tring station (London Euston to Milton Keynes) the nearest. The Beacon is about three miles from Tring station (which itself is two miles from Tring). The small extra cost of a taxi is worthwhile; to walk would mean taking the Ridgeway path and retracing your steps back to the station, which is on the route.

For those interested in Ridgeway avifauna I recommend carrying a pair of binoculars. Apart from the extensive bird life described in Chapter 4, red kites have been reintroduced in the Chilterns and have successfully established themselves between Wendover and the river Thames.

Ivinghoe Beacon to Wendover   11 miles
From the summit trig point start due south along a broad footpath which undulates to meet a road on a sharp bend. Cross this road and take the footpath uphill opposite to walk through hawthorn and blackthorn until the first right-hand stile takes you off the increasingly muddy bridleway to a field; from here there are views of Pitstone Hill with Incombe Hole in the foreground. Keep on downhill, crossing another stile, back to the original track, around Incombe Hole, over stiles and across a field to a road. Cross here, go left along the lane for 75 yards and over a stile by a fence. Follow the broad path around The Pimple, uphill and bearing left to the top of Pitstone Hill. From the top of Pitstone Hill an ancient windmill can be seen in the field across the road below. Follow the left-hand fence to a sharp left-hand turn. Stop here and note the Bridgewater Monument visible half-left sticking up through the beech trees of Ashridge across the valley. The Duke of Bridgewater, father of inland waterways, is commemorated here overlooking the summit of the Grand Union Canal at Tring.

From the corner take a small path half-right steeply downhill to a stile. Go over the stile and follow the path through beech woods to Aldbury Nowers, famous for its butterflies. The large number of fallen beech trees in this wood were victims of the October 1987 hurricane.

After descending a flight of about forty wooden steps followed by

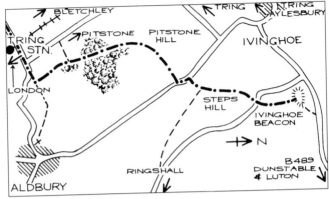

1 (westwards). Ivinghoe Beacon to Tring station.

another flight of six to a crossing path, turn right, and in 150 yards, left and continue with a right-hand fence along the edge of a wood. The path then turns right downhill to join a wide concrete drive. Continue downhill to a road, turn right into the road and continue on to Tring railway station, past the former Royal Hotel (now converted to residences) to the canal bridge. Stop here awhile and note the depth of the cutting which was dug by 'navvies' using only hand tools to dig and horses to remove the spoil. This is the highest point of the London to Birmingham Grand Union Canal opened in 1805.

Continue over the bridge and take the small lane on the left. In 150 yards turn right through a gate in a hedge gap and on up the field in an enclosed path through a second gate to a major road. Turn right on the footpath for 100 yards and, taking *extreme* care, cross this busy road to a gate opposite. Go through the gate and continue 50 yards to cross Tring bypass by the modern, elegant footbridge. Continue uphill through a gate to a second one on the left to a corner of a field, continue along the right-hand edge of this field to a gate on to a lane. Turn right and immediately left through another gate and follow this path through two fields and a right turn to another gate. Walk along an enclosed path, past an Ordnance Survey trig point, to a road.

Cross this road past two Rothschild cottages (note the fancy chimneys) and, ignoring the entrance to Tring Park, turn left alongside the wall of the second cottage. The path now leads through woodland along the back of Wigginton's gardens, over a drive following a fence on the right and turning sharp right to a stile and into a field. Follow the left edge of this field, over a stile, and turn right at the track, and continue on, passing Wick Farm to a lane.

38

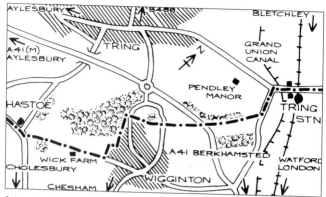

2 (westwards). Tring station to Hastoe.

At this junction follow Church Lane (signposted Hastoe) which leads to a junction, where turn left along the road. At a sharp left bend go half-right into Pavis Wood. This path continues through woodland for about three-quarters of a mile and eventually ends at a lane with a large radio aerial left. Turn left and after a few paces go right through a gate by a farmyard. Cross this field diagonally half-left to another gate by some conifers. The path then leads to a gate into another small lane.

Cross this lane and continue along the track opposite through Forestry Commission land. Deep in this wood on your right is a large stone with a plaque marking the highest point of the Chiltern Hills (SP

The footbridge across the A41.

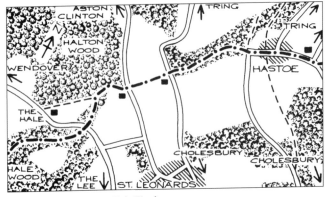

3 (westwards). Hastoe to Hale Wood.

891089). Unless visiting the summit continue on downhill between high banks to steps left leading up out of the wood to a large field. Continue to a small lane, a few yards downhill and join a path on the left through Hale Wood.

Follow this path downhill for nearly a mile keeping right where it broadens into a rough track before reaching a lane by estate gates at the end of an avenue of trees, and some farm buildings. Continue on the lane and over the crossroads after half a mile into Church Lane at Wellhead. At St Mary's church turn right into Heron Path and continue alongside a stream into Wendover High Street.

Wendover to Watlington   **16 miles**

The Ridgeway continues up Wendover High Street, over the mini roundabout and bridge over railway and bypass to a sharp right-hand bend in the road. Cross here and join a path which divides immediately. Take the central path, up Bacombe Hill, and climb through the trees, eventually reaching the memorial to the South Africa campaign 1899–1902 on the top of Coombe Hill. There are views of Aylesbury Vale and several large mansions: north-east is Halton House, built by Lord Rothschild and now RAF Halton's officers' mess; to the left of this and nearly on the horizon is Mentmore Towers, once home of Lord Rosebery; to the north-west, surrounded by trees, is nineteenth-century Waddesdon Manor, built in French château style by Baron Ferdinand de Rothschild. Chequers, country home of the prime minister of the day, can just be seen south-west. In front of the war memorial is a plinth with pointers to other places of interest.

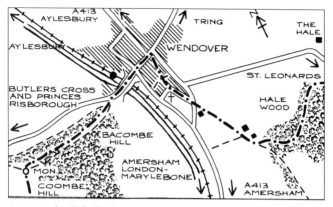

4 (westwards). Hale Wood to Coombe Hill.

Turn left at the monument and, with a golf course down below to the right, at a wire fence bear left to a gate. Go through the gate and into a wood for about 500 yards to a road. Turn right at the road and in 100 yards go through another gate on the left, soon crossing a stile and following the clearly waymarked path through a wood.

At the end of the left-hand field cross the right-hand stile and continue. Soon bear right at a crossing track and go downhill. Over the next crossing track continue straight on with fields either side to the road at Buckmoorend. Chequers is now clearly visible right and the gate over the road leads to a clearly marked path through the estate.

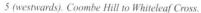

5 (westwards). Coombe Hill to Whiteleaf Cross.

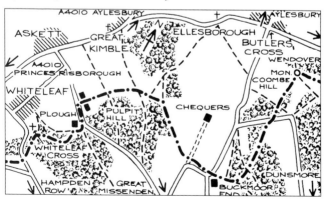

The path crossing in front of Chequers.

The fine avenue of beech trees was planted by Sir Winston Churchill and aptly named Victory Drive. The path then crosses a field to the left-hand corner of the wood opposite and turns right along the edge of the wood with Chequers still visible to the right.

Pass through the gate on the left after about 600 yards, and go across the *centre* of the field to an old iron farm gate with gate alongside, and go through this gate to the head of a valley, ignoring the crossing path. At a fork take the higher path, crossing a ditch and going past a small rounded hill on your right to a gate; go downhill for a short way then half-left to a gate.

Walk straight across this grassy clearing to another gate, continue on for a short way, then take the right turn and at once go left to enter a field. Cross the middle of this field to a gate on to a flight of steps running steeply downhill to a road with a golf course opposite. Turn left and continue to the Plough public house at Cadsden. Ignore the public footpath before the pub and take the bridleway to the right just past it, then soon fork left for the steep climb uphill to the top of Whiteleaf Hill. At your feet immediately in front of you is Whiteleaf Cross carved out of the chalk; the town below is Princes Risborough. Continue on the path to pass a picnic area and small car park, left, to the road. Here turn right for 20 yards and take the concrete drive left up to a nature reserve, following round left at the top where it ends. Keep forward with woods left, and forward alongside a single line of trees to a roadside gate. Do not go through it but turn sharp right on a grassy track down across the hillside field to a gate, then down a steep path with steps through scrub and on at the left edge of a field to a

WENDOVER TO WATLINGTON

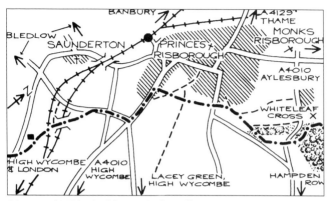

6 (westwards). Whiteleaf Cross to Lodge Hill.

track. Turn left at this track, Upper Icknield Way, over a road and
continue forward, downhill, to a busy main road. Turn left here for half
a mile to crossroads, at which point take the lane signposted to
Bledlow. Go forward over the next crossroads, and just beyond a
house, left, enter a field on the left through a hedge gap.

Ignoring the bridlepath running beside the left-hand hedge of this
field, keep right briefly before cutting across, half-left, to a gate
midway between the two pylons. Pass through the gate, going over one
end of a railway tunnel, a field, then another (but unguarded) railway
line, with more gates. Follow the hedge-lined path through a golf
course to a gate, then across a field to a house and on to a road. Cross

7 (westwards). Lodge Hill to Chinnor.

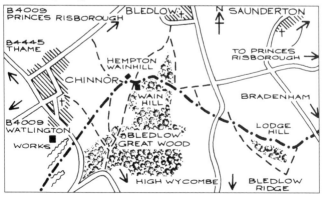

43

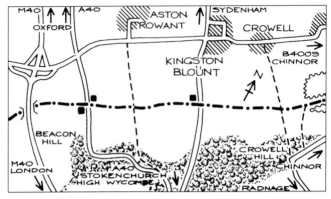

8 (westwards). Chinnor to Beacon Hill.

the road into a field opposite, following its left-hand edge to the far corner. Go through a hedge gap and continue straight on through gates and uphill towards the top of Lodge Hill, veering to the right along the top of the grassy ridge. Descend through scrub, follow a left-hand hedge, then go left through a gate and across two fields to a road. Go through the gate opposite and along the left edge of a field and, ignoring a stile, through a left-hand gate before the end of the field into another field. Keep to the right edge of this field for 400 yards, then bear left towards a gate on to the Upper Icknield Way. Turn left through the beech wood, passing a wooden lodge, right, and later a cottage, left. Here, at Hempton Wainhill, the path turns left and presently passes a picnic area and two houses with a tennis court.

Continue, crossing the Chinnor road, then, after one and a half miles, the road to Kingston Blount by an old railway-crossing keeper's cottage. Go forward for another mile to the busy A40 road, continuing along the lower slopes of Beacon Hill.

The Ridgeway, very wide now, passes via a tunnel under the M40 motorway and goes across open countryside (and two crossing tracks) for three miles to the B480 Watlington road by a bungalow. The Ridgeway continues opposite but to reach the old market town of Watlington turn right here and follow the road downhill.

Watlington to Goring   14 miles

To regain the Ridgeway from the centre of Watlington, leave by Hill Road; in 400 yards, just beyond house number 90, the Ridgeway crosses the road. Turn right on to the path and in about half a mile the way crosses the B480 road to continue on a lane leading to a multi-path junction. There is a permissive footpath here as an alternative to

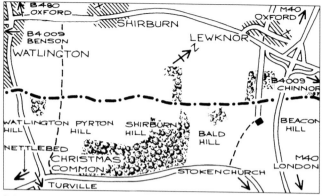

9 (westwards). Beacon Hill to Watlington.

the road. Keep straight on between hedges and past some large houses on your left, and eventually, after some open ground, meet a road. Cross this road and resume on the track opposite until a left-hand farm track between farm buildings and a row of trees. Take this path uphill to a fork just before a wood and take the right-hand route along the edge of the wood. Soon the path swings left and into the wood and then downhill to run alongside a field, then rises again to meet a road. Proceed forward along this road a short way to the interesting Norman church at Swyncombe. After a visit to the church leave by passing the church on your left and going through a gate and along a path which bears right. Ignore a left-hand gate but in 100 yards, where the path

10 (westwards). Watlington to Swyncombe.

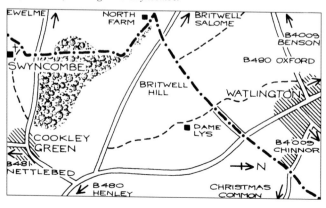

Westwards from Swyncombe church.

divides, climb a left-hand stile uphill to a wood, emerging at the corner of a field. Follow around the left-hand edge of the field to a green path. This farm track will take you to Ewelme Park Farm, where a left turn between the farm buildings along the side of the house should be taken. After 200 yards the path forks; take the left-hand track. In 20 yards the path forks again. This time follow the right-hand path to the edge of the wood and a large field. The public footpath crosses the centre of this field to a white post opposite and enters a small wood, then crosses another field to another white post, this time right of centre. At this point the path leads uphill through trees to a gate on Gangsdown Hill by the A4130 road.

Cross over this busy road. The Ridgeway passes in front of the cottages opposite and goes left alongside the last one (Fairway Cottage). The footpath now crosses a golf course and has been marked by the greenkeepers by a series of white, numbered posts. Keep a careful eye out for golfers and golf balls while crossing several fairways! The path enters a wood and then crosses further fairways. The last marker post is by the club house car park.

From the car park the path crosses a small field to meet a narrow lane by Nuffield church. A sign by the church gate offers the use of the water tap on the church wall for thirsty walkers and their dogs.

Pass the church on your left and soon go through a hedge gap to a field giving extensive views over the Thames valley (spoiled only by the intrusive cooling towers of Didcot power station). Follow the left

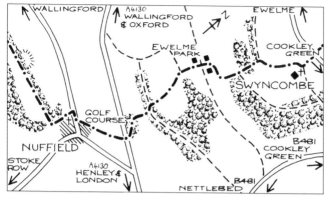

11 (westwards). Swyncombe to Nuffield.

edge of this field to the far corner and begin a long downhill stretch alongside Grim's Ditch walking under trees on a raised bank, crossing several stiles and two minor roads until after about three miles the busy A4074 has to be crossed.

Having safely crossed the A4074, go right for 30 yards and enter Mongewell Park via a gate. This small path runs through woodland, parallel to the noisy Wallingford bypass, to another gate. Turn left here along a paved path to the drive of Carmel College. Keep on the drive past academic buildings and private residences to a path, with a field left, which leaves the college grounds and leads past a golf course to the village of North Stoke. Walk through the village and turn right at

12 (westwards). Nuffield to Mongewell Park .

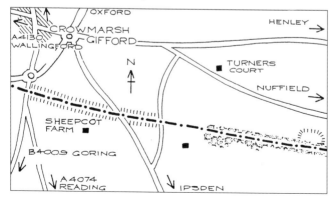

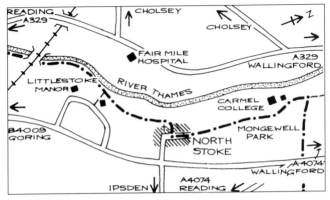

13 (westwards). Mongewell Park to South Stoke.

a junction into Church Lane. Pass around the right side of the church through the churchyard to a gate. The path now crosses, between laurel hedges, the lawn of a garden and continues through flood meadows separated by gates, with the Thames flowing in the same direction on your right. Continue past the side of a house to a crossing path. Turn right here and after a few yards arrive at the river bank, where turn left past a Second World War pill box.

The path now follows the river downstream for about a mile through gates and under a four-arched, skewed railway bridge (protected by another pill box) until, shortly after you reach a gravelled path, the village of Moulsford comes into view across the river. Here the path

14 (westwards). South Stoke to Goring.

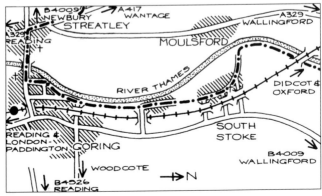

Goring Lock on the river Thames.

turns left, leaving the river for a while, to the small village of South
Stoke. Keep on through the village, past the thirteenth-century church,
the primary school and the Perch and Pike public house until the road
bends left and goes under a railway bridge. Here leave the road and go
straight on, taking the bridlepath across a field to a road and the
outskirts of Goring. At a sharp left-hand bend just before a railway
bridge go straight on along a bridleway for half a mile to another road.
Proceed up this road past the drive to the Leathern Bottle and take a
wide path high above the river and alongside the railway line. Join
Cleeve Road and continue on to Clevemede. Here take a small path on

15 (westwards). Goring to Warren Farm.

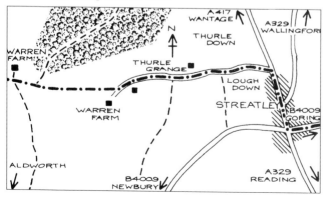

49

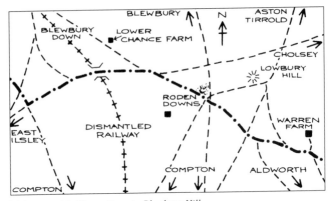

16 (westwards). Warren Farm to Blewbury Hill.

the right opposite Clevemede, a small cul-de-sac of large houses, and downhill into the centre of Goring and the bridge over the river Thames.

Goring to Wantage   16 miles

This section of the walk is about sixteen miles across the Berkshire and Oxfordshire Downs and does not pass any shops; the only refreshment available is a water tap at about halfway on Several Down just before crossing under the busy A34.

Having crossed the Thames into Streatley, follow the road to the traffic lights at the top of the hill. Here turn right along the A329 for about 300 yards, then cross the road and take the left fork (A417). After another 300 yards, turn left along Rectory Road by a letter box. Soon you will pass a golf course on your left with fields on the right. This road gradually becomes more and more rural until after one and a half miles at another letter box at Warren Farm it ends in a drive to the farm and a broad track leading uphill to your right. Take this track, ignoring all side tracks and paths, across Roden Down. After a mile the track descends and widens into a double track which is heavily rutted; extra care should be taken to avoid twisting an ankle. After another mile the path crosses the disused track of the Didcot, Newbury and Southampton Railway and climbs again to a crossway with a concrete drive. Turn right here and stay on the concrete drive until it sweeps left through gates by a drinking fountain. A plaque on the stone by the tap reads: 'In memory of Dr Basil Phillips LVO 1914–1995. General practitioner Newbury and district 1945–1979. He was a country man.' The Ridgeway resumes as an unmade track again which soon follows the rails of a horse gallop at Several Down.

Having resumed the path after a well-earned break, keep a lookout

50

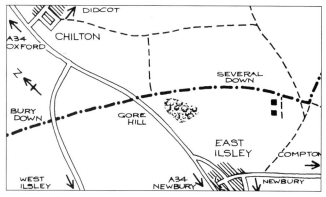

17 (westwards). Blewbury Hill to Bury Down.

just before the A34 underpass on the right for a monument to a young soldier who died here. 'Near this spot, Hugh Frederick Grosvenor, 2nd Lieutenant, The Life Guards, lost his life in an armoured car accident while on military duty 9th April 1947 Aged 19 years.'

The A34 underpass is soon reached and has been brightened up with murals of local historical events by the Compton Art Group: 'Beaker Folly 3000 BC', 'Battle of Ashdown AD 871', 'Alfred defeats the Danes' etc. There is even a rhyme:

Ilsley remote amid the Berkshire Downs
Claims three distinctions o'er her sister towns;

18 (westwards). Bury Down to Wantage monument.

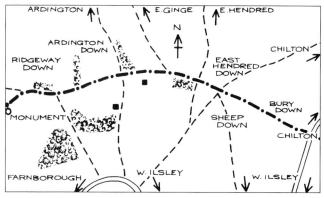

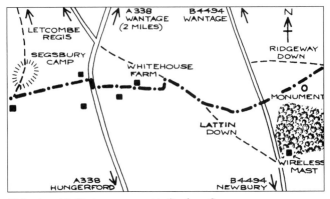

19 (westwards). Wantage monument to Segsbury Camp.

Far famed for sheep and wool though not for spinners,
For sportsmen, doctors, publicans and sinners.

After the underpass follow the broad path across Bury Down, with views of Harwell Research Establishment and Didcot power station, to a crossing after a mile with the road to West Ilsley. Cross this road and continue for another mile, passing through a car park. In another two miles the path leads uphill to another monument, this time in honour of Lord Wantage, awarded the Victoria Cross in the Crimean War, 1854. In a further half mile cross the B4494 road and continue straight on. Where the path turns left in 200 yards, carry straight on again across Lattin Down, and at a junction with a gravelled road, and a sign to Court House Ridgeway Centre, turn left and follow a farm track leading past Whitehouse Farm to the main A338 road to Wantage, where you turn right along the road for 30 yards to a letterbox and house and the trail again.

Wantage to Wanborough Plain   12 miles

Setting off from the A338 junction with the Ridgeway, the firm farm road gives way to two miles that are heavily rutted and muddy in wet weather. After a short distance, Segsbury Camp, Iron Age in origin, is passed on the right. Ignore the track and road leading right to Letcombe Bassett at Gramp's Hill and continue on downhill for a mile, passing Folly Clump, an isolated group of beech trees on the left, and passing south of Crowhole Bottom and Devil's Punchbowl. In another mile, cross the B4001 and continue along the metalled road 400 yards further, where the farm track goes off to the left, opposite for 100 yards, where the Ridgeway resumes as a track. There is another

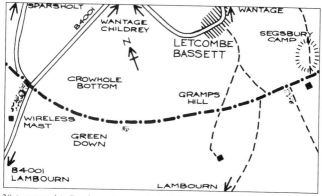

20 (westwards). Segsbury Camp to Crowhole Bottom.

drinking tap and animal trough here with a small memorial announcing: 'This tap is placed here in memory of Peter Wren aged 14 years. He loved the countryside.'

After half a mile the path reaches a crossing track; continue on to the Kingston Lisle road at Blowingstone Hill. (The stone, for those who wish to visit it, stands beside a cottage at the foot of the hill half a mile distant.) The Ridgeway climbs steadily now for nearly two miles to the next landmark – White Horse Hill, topped by the impressive earthworks of Uffington Castle; the White Horse of Uffington, cut out of the turf, is just over the brow of the hill. The Ridgeway now sweeps on for mile and a half to the next attraction, Wayland's Smithy. This neolithic

21 (westwards). Crowhole Bottom to White Horse Hill.

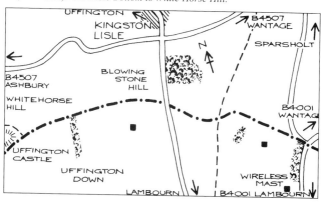

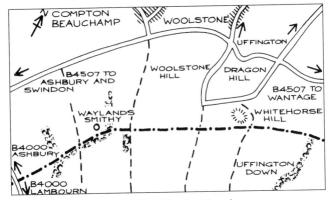

22 (westwards). White Horse Hill to Kingstone Coombes.

long barrow, surrounded by trees, is perhaps the most famous landmark of the Ridgeway and attracts many thousands of visitors annually.

A further half mile after crossing the B4000 the Ridgeway crosses a farm track at the aptly named Ridgeway Farm and passes from Oxfordshire into Wiltshire.

After another mile or so now, again straight on, the Ridgeway is interrupted abruptly at a T junction by a minor road. From this point to Wanborough walkers have to endure a mile or so of road walking. Turn left downhill from the T junction to the Shepherd's Rest public house, continue straight over the crossroads and follow the lane to a

23 (westwards). Kingstone Coombes to Fox Hill.

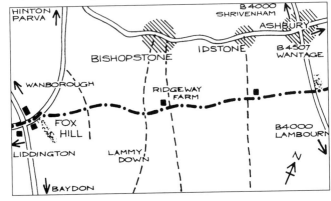

Wayland's Smithy.

small side road just before the M4. Here, those staying on the Ridgeway continue on uphill over the M4 to the B4192, while those leaving the Ridgeway route for Wanborough turn right and follow this lane to Wanborough village.

Wanborough Plain to Overton Hill   16 miles

At the B4192 turn left and follow the verge to the Ridgeway signpost 200 yards on. Go through the gate and climb the signposted path, past a Second World War pillbox on the right, on to Liddington Hill, where the earthworks of Iron Age Liddington Castle come into

24 (westwards). Fox Hill to Upham.

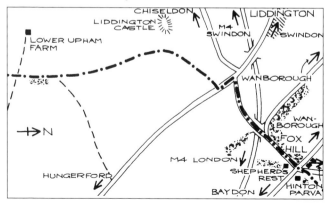

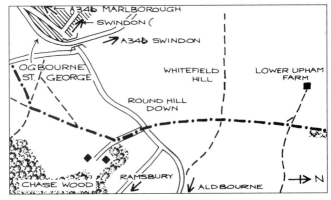

25 (westwards). Upham to Round Hill Down.

view as you approach the summit. The path, however, veers away just before reaching the castle, curving left to a gate, and soon follows a hedgerow for a short distance before breaking into familiar open country again. The path now skirts several large fields, crossing two major paths, for a mile and a half before reaching the Aldbourne to Ogbourne road. Here cross to the lane opposite and continue for 400 yards to the edge of a wood, where the lane bends left by a water tower, and take the track half-right for about three quarters of a mile to a crossing track by a derelict brick building. Turn right here and follow the path downhill, bearing left and crossing over a minor road and continuing downhill between the piers of a derelict railway bridge to

26 (westwards). Round Hill Down to Coombe Down.

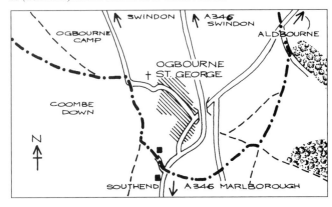

56

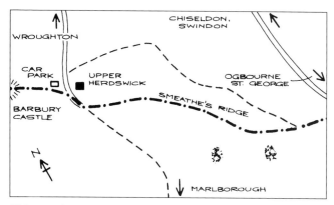

27 (westwards). Coombe Down to Barbury Castle.

some thatched cottages by the A345 road at Southend.

Take the 'No through road' opposite, signposted Hallam, and cross the river Og where the lane changes to a stony track. Turn right at a T junction along a small path to another road. Go along the road for 100 yards, then turn uphill on a concrete drive which soon deteriorates into a rough track. Where the track divides at a gate and stile take the left-hand branch and after a short while start climbing up on to Smeathe's Ridge overlooking a deep valley.

Follow the path across the ridge for a mile, passing a seat placed in memory of a local rambler, until a T junction at Upper Herdswick Farm. Turn right here and take a left turn opposite the farm towards

28 (westwards). Barbury Castle to Rough Hill.

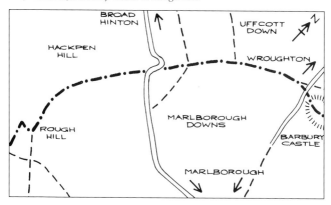

57

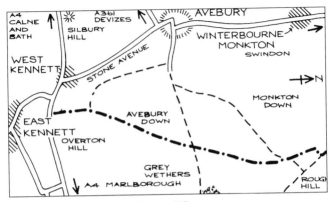

29 (westwards). Rough Hill to Overton Hill.

Iron Age Barbury Castle. This large and very impressive earthwork attracts many visitors, who are now catered for at Barbury Castle Country Park, with car park, toilets, visitor centre and information displays. Passing through a gate, complete with a blunt 'Dogs will be shot' notice, the Ridgeway cuts right through the centre of the castle and drops downhill to a junction. One and a half miles ahead across the Marlborough Downs the Broad Hinton to Marlborough road is crossed before the ascent of Hackpen Hill (892 feet) with its clumps of beech trees. Walk onwards across Fyfield Down, negotiating a sharp right and left turn and then passing a low standing stone beside the path. This is good for resting and is one of several sarsen stones, called grey wethers, in the vicinity. Continue on, passing the entrance to Fyfield Down Nature Reserve. From here Avebury can be seen below to the right as the Ridgeway makes its way through numerous barrows (crowned with stands of beech trees planted by the Victorians) and other reminders of its ancient origins until the end is reached, pointing in the same direction, due south, as it started on Ivinghoe Beacon eighty-five miles ago. Here it meets the modern A4 at Overton Hill, by a nondescript car park.

On the opposite side of the A4 are the remains of a neolithic circle called The Sanctuary which was once linked by the Kennett Avenue of standing stones to Avebury two miles west. Unfortunately there is no bus stop or telephone box at Overton Hill. The nearest are at West Kennett, half a mile west downhill on the busy A4. Here buses can be caught to Avebury or Marlborough and there is a red BT call box for telephoning taxis.

3
The archaeology of the Ridgeway
by James Dyer

No one proposing to follow the Ridgeway eastwards should fail to visit the little village of Avebury (SU 103699) before commencing their walk, if only to placate the ancient British gods who will be accompanying them for most of the journey. Most people will agree that the great stone circle at Avebury, with its surrounding ditch and bank, must once have formed a temple or religious centre for the neolithic farmers of the north Wiltshire downs. It was here, perhaps, that they practised their spring and harvest celebrations, made their laws and dispensed justice. The Avebury circle, which is the largest in western Europe, is dominated by the massive earthworks of the bank and internal ditch enclosing 29 acres and more than 1140 feet in diameter. The great ditch was 30 feet deep after excavation and probably separated the laity from their priests or elders who performed the internal ceremonies. This earthwork was built between 2900 and 2800 BC. Near its centre two small circles of stones were erected shortly afterwards. About 2500 BC an outer ring of ninety-eight massive sarsen stones, some weighing as much as forty tons, were set up, as well as two long avenues of stones, one leading south to The Sanctuary (see below) and a second (now destroyed) west towards Beckhampton. The Avebury story, together with that of the neighbouring monuments, can be best understood by following a path through the churchyard which leads to the excellent site museum.

The archaeology of the Ridgeway path begins immediately that one steps on to it, for its present course begins on Seven Barrow Hill (or Overton Hill as the maps call it), one and a half miles south-east of Avebury village. Only six of the original seven burial mounds survive on the hill. One south of the A4 contained a burial in a tree-trunk coffin, whilst north of the road (SU 119682) are three bell-barrows and two bowl barrows of Bronze Age date. Most of these were excavated by William Cunnington at the beginning of the nineteenth century and contained cremations, some with bronze daggers.

Also at the start of the Ridgeway is a small stone and timber circle called The Sanctuary (SU 118679), which was excavated by a later member of the Cunnington family, Maud, in 1930. This consisted of six concentric rings of wooden posts and two rings of stones, all apparently free standing. Both posts and stones have now disappeared and their places have been indicated with concrete markers. The purpose of the site was unknown but was probably religious or astronomical. A reconsideration of the excavation suggests that it was built about 2500 BC and that the burial of a boy with a drinking vessel beside one of the stones was added a century later. The Sanctuary was connected to Avebury by an avenue of large sarsen stones which ran down the hill and then turned north-west for a distance of nearly two miles before reaching the great stone circle.

The sarsen stones (sarsen maybe a corruption of *saracen*, a foreigner) were almost certainly dragged down to Avebury from the Marlborough Downs beside the Ridgeway path. Many more of these can be seen in the nature reserve at the eastern end of the bridlepath from Avebury on the Overton and Fyfield Downs (SU 135710). One of the stones in the reserve has grooves in its surface, made when neolithic man polished his stone axes (SU 128715). The stones are locally known as grey wethers since from a distance they tend to look like sheep. There are some fine Celtic fields in the nature reserve, as well as the British Association's experimental archaeological earthwork constructed in 1960.

As the Ridgeway proceeds northwards one can see the low mound of Windmill Hill two and a half miles to the west (SU 087714), which gives its name to an important causewayed enclosure dating from around 3300 BC. Its uses probably included settlement and corral, a market and exchange centre and a mortuary area for the exposure of corpses. Soon, below the walker, on the side of Hackpen Hill is a small white horse carved into the hillside to commemorate Queen Victoria's coronation in 1838.

The path curves to the east when it reaches Barbury Castle (SU 149763), a strong Iron Age hillfort with double ramparts and ditches. Aerial photographs show that it contained huts and storage pits, whilst excavations by Colt Hoare in the early nineteenth century found chariot fittings and pottery. There is a boundary dyke of the same date immediately east of the fort, whilst Burderop Down to the north has extensive traces of Celtic fields on it.

The path descends to Ogbourne St George and then climbs again to Round Hill Downs, where there are more prehistoric boundary dykes and traces of Iron Age settlement, running for three miles to Liddington Castle (SU 209797), a small oval hillfort with a single line of defence around the hilltop. Excavations have shown that the rampart, originally of timber and turf, was later heightened with dumped chalk obtained by enlarging the ditch. Originally built with entrances to west and east, the former was later blocked off. In the south-western quarter of the fort the top of an apparent ritual shaft has been located but only partially excavated. The fort was probably occupied between the seventh and fifth centuries BC.

After a mile of road, we continue along the Ridgeway with strip lynchets representing ancient field systems on the escarpment to the north. Three quarters of a mile after crossing the B4000 a clump of

Barbury Castle.

trees on the left tells us that we have arrived at Wayland's Smithy (SU 281854), a chambered long barrow constructed about 3400 BC. At its southern end is a short stone-lined passage with a small burial chamber on either side The one on the left contained about eight burials when it was opened in 1919. Re-excavation in 1962-3 showed that the chambered barrow lay over the top of an earlier mound which had covered a wooden burial chamber containing fourteen burials. This earlier neolithic barrow can no longer be seen. It was dated to about 3700 BC.

The Ridgeway continues eastwards and the hill crest ahead is soon dominated by the ramparts of another Iron Age hillfort, Uffington Castle (SU 299864). A single rampart originally built of chalk and timber in the seventh century BC was later heightened and topped by a sarsen stone breastwork. It is broken by an original entrance facing north-west. Two breaks in the north and south ramparts were made in Roman times. On the slope of the hill to the north is the most celebrated chalk-cut hill figure in England, the White Horse of Uffington (SU 302866). This was thought by many to represent an Iron Age tribal symbol, and by others to be of Saxon date, but a new dating method known as optically stimulated luminescence was applied to material excavated from the foundations of the horse in 1994. This suggests that it was cut in the late Bronze Age, between 1400 and 600 BC. Below the horse, the curious flat-topped Dragon Hill is the traditional spot where St George slew the dragon.

Nothing can be seen of the fort which once stood on Rams Hill. At the foot of Blowingstone Hill is a naturally perforated block of sarsen in a cottage garden (SU 324871) which can be blown to make a loud siren-like sound. Tradition says that King Alfred blew it to summon the Saxons to battle against the Danes.

Passing a round barrow on the left as the path crosses the B4001, the Ridgeway continues next to Segsbury Camp (SU 385845), a hillfort of 25 acres. Excavation has shown that it was originally defended by a wooden stockade, backed by a chalk and turf bank. Later this was rebuilt with crude drystone walling to make a box-rampart. Later still this was incorporated into a massive dumped chalk rampart with a sarsen wall at its rear. The V-shaped external ditch was 26 feet wide and 13 feet deep. Limited work inside the fort has revealed the footings of two round houses and forty storage pits.

The Berkshire Grim's Ditch which lies north of our path for the next few miles probably formed a territorial boundary in the Iron Age. There are a number of barrows on this section of the downs, some with names like Scutchamer Knoll (SU 456850) and Fox Barrow (SU 506831) near Churn Farm.

A small rectangular banked enclosure on Lowbury Hill (SU 540823) dates from the Roman period. Opinions differ as to whether it was a temple or a farmstead. The skeleton of a woman, apparently murdered, was found under the wall in the south-west corner, and it is suggested that she might have been a dedicatory sacrifice.

Before leaving the Ridgeway on top of the Downs notice the twin hilltops of the Sinodun Hills seven miles to the north. The right-hand one is crowned with yet another hillfort, seemingly guarding the river Thames crossing as it enters the hill country.

The path now descends to Goring and we enter Chiltern country. There are no antiquities to be seen as we walk beside the Thames, but the curious may care to divert two miles to the east to the village of Ipsden, where in a copse behind the school is a splendid folly, a stone circle known as The Devil's Ninepins, erected in 1827, and incorporating a number of sarsen stones, the largest of which took nine horses to move (SU 633851).

From Mongewell Park to Nuffield the path follows the Mongewell Grim's Ditch (SU 608883 to SU 682868), an earthwork five miles long, stretching from the flood plain of the river up to the clay-capped hilltops to the east. The bank, which faces south, seems to block progress along the Icknield Way. It may date from the end of the Iron Age and was probably constructed to divide one tribal territory from another. The path zigzags northwards, passing the Norman church at Swyncombe, and up to another earthwork on top of Swyncombe Down, which may be a late Bronze Age ranch boundary (SU 675915). Shortly after this the path joins the Icknield Way, the major prehistoric route connecting central England with East Anglia.

At Watlington the path passes beneath the White Mark (SU

700939), an obelisk design cut into the chalk of the hillside by Edward Horne in 1764 to form a landscape feature in his estate. On the side of Bald Hill are a number of deep and ancient traffic ruts cutting into the hillside and marking the course of former roads (SU 725963), and similar ruts can be seen on the south-western side of Beacon Hill, above the motorway.

For those who would climb up on to the hills above Chinnor there are two round barrows enclosed by a single ditch (SP 767006) on the open hillside, and another called the Cop in the trees on Wain Hill (SP 773011). Excavation suggested a Bronze Age date for the latter, though a good case has been made for considering it Saxon. Also on Wain Hill is the Bledlow Cross (SP 769009), another figure cut into the chalk, probably at the end of the eighteenth century.

Between the Cuttle Brook and the railway track (SP 769017) ploughing has produced tiles, pottery and coins which point to the presence of a Roman building, as yet unexcavated. Nothing is visible of the small Roman villa excavated in the late 1930s east of Saunderton church.

The footpath now crosses the Risborough gap and passes along the northern side of Lodge Hill. Between the path and the hill lie two ploughed bell-barrows of the Bronze Age (SP 789004). These can still be seen as dark marks in the freshly ploughed soil or rings in the growing corn and have produced flint implements and pieces of beaker pottery. There are traces of hut circles and enclosure ditches on Lodge Hill itself.

After following the A4010 for half a mile the path turns north-east along the edge of Princes Risborough. Ploughed-out strip lynchets can be seen across the valley to the south (SP 810023). The path now climbs steeply into the woods and comes out above the Whiteleaf Cross (SP 822040). This large hill-carving of a cross surmounting a pyramid is almost 250 feet high. Like many of the other hill figures, its origin is uncertain. It seems most likely to have been cut at the beginning of the eighteenth century, though it might conceivably be connected with Missenden Abbey, dissolved in 1539. Above the cross are the excavated remains of the Whiteleaf barrow (also SP 822040), a kidney-shaped neolithic burial mound opened in the 1930s and found to contain a wooden burial chamber and the burial of a middle-aged man, together with pieces of more than fifty pots. There is a second, unexcavated barrow at the northern end of the ridge (SP 821043) and, between the two, the low mound for a windmill with a cross-shaped depression in its surface.

A mile further north-east is the small unexcavated Iron Age hillfort of Pulpit Hill (SP 832050). A track branches right from the Ridgeway at SP 830054 and climbs directly to the fort, which is roughly square in plan with a double line of rampart and ditch on the east. The rest of

Ivinghoe Beacon.

the hill is defended by a single line of rampart. This is the first hillfort we have seen since we crossed the Thames, a distance of almost twenty-two miles. There are ancient agricultural boundaries, perhaps of the Iron Age, in the adjoining woods.

There are two burial mounds on Bacombe Hill as the path approaches Wendover (SP 862072); one appears to be a bell-barrow and there may be a pond-barrow on its south side.

There is an overgrown hillfort on Boddington Hill above Wendover (SP 882020), which enthusiasts may wish to examine. Approached along the forestry path from the Wendover–Hale road, the fort has a single rampart and ditch and encloses about 17 acres. A little south of the Ridgeway path at Hale Wood is a good section of the Chiltern Grim's Ditch (SP 901073). This boundary ditch runs for many miles through the Chilterns and seems to have marked a territorial boundary at some time during the late Iron Age.

There are extensive earthworks on the hills beyond Tring station which include further sections of the Grim's Ditch at Aldbury Nowers and Pitstone Hill. The ditch is well seen sweeping around the end of Pitstone Hill (SP 950142) and bending to avoid a group of three possible neolithic flint mines, the tops of whose shafts and waste heaps can be clearly seen. There are other earthworks on this hill which are as yet unexcavated and undated.

Three miles north-west beyond the former cement works Southend Hill at Cheddington is clearly visible. Aerial photographs have shown this to be ringed with what appears to be yet another (ploughed-out) Chiltern hillfort of some 12.3 acres.

The path now runs to its final extremity as it follows the Icknield Way along the flank of Steps Hill and round the south side of Ivinghoe Beacon. Every minor hilltop here is crowned with a barrow, and the Beacon itself is ringed with a hillfort, pear-shaped in plan, and shown by excavation to be one of the earliest in England, dating back to at least 700 BC. Its entrance lay at the eastern end (SP 960168) and there were traces of huts in a sheltered hollow in the south-east side when it was excavated between 1963 and 1965. Other huts have been found on a narrow platform on the scarp of the hill, outside the northern rampart. A fine Wilburton-style bronze sword dated to *c*.1150–950 BC was found inside the fort in 2000. A geophysical survey of the interior suggested there might once have been a neolithic mortuary enclosure, where corpses were exposed to the elements, on the hilltop. There is a worn-down round barrow on the summit of the Beacon, a few yards south of the triangulation pillar. From this viewpoint can be seen the Dunstable Downs to the east with the White Lion of Whipsnade (1933) and the Five Knolls barrow cemetery above Dunstable.

Our path ends here, but the Icknield Way continues along the Chilterns and for another hundred miles until it reaches the sea near Hunstanton. Many miles of its Norfolk length follow trackways similar to the Ridgeway path and pass the magnificent neolithic flint mines at Grimes Graves (Brandon). Some of you may be tempted to see it through to the end.

4
The natural history of the Ridgeway
by A. C. Fraser

The Ridgeway path follows, with some diversions, the northern escarpment of the chalk mass formed in the Cretaceous periods of the Mesozoic era, close to the meeting of chalk and upper greensand. In some areas the chalk is covered with deposits, varying in depth, of gravels and clay-with-flints which add variety to the plant life. The type of vegetation along the walk has been greatly influenced by the activities of farmers, but for whose past methods of management we should have to walk through shrubs and trees. Until the eighteenth century sheep had been pastured on the downland as far back as neolithic times, and these flocks were of vast numbers. During the early years of the eighteenth century more and more of the downland was brought under cultivation for growing cereals, and by the end of the Napoleonic Wars the Ridgeway was a patchwork of grazing lands mixed with arable fields. These latter were later abandoned and overrun by scrub until the First World War, when they were again cultivated. Between the two world wars, many fields were allowed to revert to scrub and much of the land on the Lambourn Downs was taken over as gallops for racehorses. During the Second World War ploughing took place again on a very extensive scale and what we now see along the Wiltshire, Oxfordshire and Berkshire section of the Ridgeway walk is a mixture of scrub, grasslands, arable and racing gallops.

The turf which provides such a springy walking surface is formed by grasses which send out lateral shoots which, if they are not grazed, produce leaves and then erect flowering stalks. Grazing prevents the development of the flowering stalks, and more and more shoots appear at the base of the plants which interweave with each other and form the close turf which the sheep keep down to about two inches. Until their numbers were decimated by myxomatosis, rabbits infested some areas and ate down the turf so closely that it was useless for sheep or cattle. Many species of grasses make up the downland turf, sheep's fescue and red fescue being dominant. Apart from the grasses, chalk grassland has characteristic herbs, many of which have bright flowers. Salad burnet, whose young leaves both smell and taste like cucumber, and small scabious, with its bluish-lilac flowers, are widespread. The lovely-scented wild thyme, the stemless thistle, with its rosette of very prickly leaves and crimson flower, the tiny white flowers of fairy flax, and the umbelliferous burnet saxifrage are all constant species. Bird's-foot-trefoil, hairy hawkbit, ribwort plantain and red clover also occur freely in downland pastures.

Near Avebury, on Fyfield Down, one sees a wilderness of stones lying prostrate with only a few juniper bushes scattered amongst them. These are sarsen stones and their distinct resemblance to a flock of sheep has earned them the name of grey wethers. They consist of hard sandstone and are used to form the circles at Avebury. They are the main materials used in the construction of Wayland's Smithy and other long barrows and later appeared in village buildings. In the eighteen miles where the Ridgeway is 'laid like a green fillet across the brow' of the escarpment in Oxfordshire and Berkshire the way is impressively wide, sometimes 30 yards or more. It is often bounded by banks tangled with thorn, maple, spindle, bryony, traveller's joy and occasional beeches. The trackway itself is dominated by upright brome grass and the coarser members of the chalk flora, including pyramidal orchid, dropwort, greater knapweed, restharrow, melilot and eyebright, the last being one of a group of plants which are partially parasitic as they obtain some of their food from other plants by means of attachments from their roots to those of their hosts. The dense mass of the roots of grasses in downland turf provides them with very suitable conditions in which to flourish.

In spring, cowslips and violets can be found. During the summer the dominant flowers are the vetches, agrimony, the bedstraws, melilot, yellow-wort and sheepsbit. In the autumn the colours of the hedgerow leaves and berries are reinforced by the flowers of scabious, knapweed, ragwort, fennel and teasel.

One should look particularly round the ramparts of the old forts and other earthworks, for especially interesting plants are often to be found in their vicinity. White Horse Hill, despite the numbers of visitors to Uffington Castle, has a varied flora which includes the inconspicuous musk orchid, whose yellowish flowers have a strong smell of honey, candytuft, which likes open places on hill slopes, and field fleawort, which occurs in small areas spread along the ridge. On one earthwork occurs the large autumn or Chiltern gentian, which will be seen more frequently in the Chiltern part of the walk. Here in its Berkshire site it grows beside the autumn gentian and the hybrid between them was first described from this locality. The old emplacements of Grim's Ditch support many flowers.

Among the butterflies to be seen in summer, chalk-hill blues may be spotted and many of the browns, including the meadow brown, gatekeeper, wall, ringlet and small heath.

The bird life on the open downland of the Ridgeway varies greatly according to the season. Skylarks occur all along the way; during the spring and summer one can almost always hear their attractive song. Meadow pipits and corn buntings are frequently seen and heard, and, although their numbers have diminished, red-legged partridges can often be picked out in the arable fields.

During the spring and autumn migrations small parties of birds can be seen flying along the escarpment. Although these parties are usually small, the total numbers are sometimes considerable. Chaffinches, skylarks, fieldfares, redwings, linnets, goldfinches and greenfinches all occur in these movements. These migrations are mostly recorded during the autumn, the spring passage being far less conspicuous. Flocks of lapwings are almost always present, the numbers building up from October until March. Golden plover are not common but flocks should be looked for during the winter months, when lesser black-backed, herring, common and black-headed gulls also visit the area. Wood pigeons occur in large numbers; stock doves are not so numerous but the now established collared dove is increasing. None of the owls is common but the visiting short-eared owl is occasionally recorded during the winter and spring. Swifts, swallows and house martins pass overhead on many spring and autumn days. Where thickets occur, lesser whitethroats, tree pipits and other summer visitors may be found breeding. A very few whinchats breed but most of those seen are on passage, as are the wheatears and stonechats. During the winter, flocks of buntings and finches move on to the farmland. Tree sparrows only occur during the winter months when it appears that the breeding pairs from the vale move up on to the downs.

Buzzards are regularly seen, especially on the western part of the trail, and red kites are now a feature of the Chilterns. One may also see kestrels and sparrowhawks and in summer look out for a hobby and during the winter for a peregrine or merlin.

One of the most rewarding areas for chalk flowers is the slope descending to the river at Goring at the end of the Berkshire Ridgeway. There is a totally different flora as one walks along the Thames before turning up into the Chilterns. Purple loosestrife, valerian, figwort, fleabane, the willowherbs, the water-mints and comfrey are some of the most striking flowers along the riverbank. On the water, coot, moorhen and mallard are frequent and you may see a little grebe or more rarely a great crested grebe. Canada geese occur and if you are fortunate a kingfisher may flash across the water.

Turning away from the river, the path leaves the gault, Kimmeridge and Oxford clays of the fertile plain and crosses the upper greensand before reaching once again the chalk of the uplands. It is here at the foot of the scarp that the springs which nurture the watercress beds reach the surface. Walking along the banks of Grim's Ditch, which stretches like a green ribbon over the land, look for the nettle-leaved bellflower which grows along the edge of the rampart.

Along the Chiltern section of the walk there is a greater variety of plant and bird life as it passes through many woods and on occasions descends almost to the foot of the hills. On the steep escarpment slopes juniper dominates the scrub. In some places beech has grown amongst them and when the trees are big enough to cause shading the junipers die, and in some of these young beechwoods dead bushes are frequently seen. These beeches seldom grow to more than 70 feet owing to the shallow soil overlying the chalk. The long tapering Swyncombe Down, between the deep dry coombs running into the hills, has a great variety of plants, spindle being abundant. Fallow deer have often been seen on these slopes and on the downs near here is the place where stone curlew gather before their autumn migration. In the Britwell area occur musk thistle, dusky yellow fennel, which grows up to six feet, St John's-wort, harebell, rosebay, burdock and wild mignonette. On Watlington Hill there is a fine forest of yews. Lewknor Copse, a small beechwood, contains spurge laurel, an evergreen shrub which flowers from January until March, and both white and narrow-lipped helleborines. It is managed by the Berks, Bucks and Oxon Wildlife Trust to protect these rare plants. At Chinnor Hill the path runs near the Chinnor Hill Reserve owned by the Trust, which is open to all. This reserve of 65 acres is a mixture of woodland, grassland and scrub and grazing experiments are being carried out to restore more of the chalk turf. Part of the chalk is here overlaid with clay with a resulting difference in vegetation. Near here red kites were re-introduced to the countryside and are now a frequent sight in the western Chilterns.

Along the Icknield Way to Lodge Hill the path is bordered by bright flowers such as scabious, knapweed, vetches and thistles. The woods by Lower Cadsden contain white and common helleborine and, where the chalk is exposed, sheets of candytuft. Here, too, if you are lucky, you will find plants of bird's-nest orchid and yellow bird's-nest, both of which live on the decayed remains of dead leaves. They only flower at long intervals and have been recorded flowering on dates from early May until July. The earth-star fungus also occurs here. Nuthatches can be heard in these woods and both the redstart and wood warbler, summer visitors which are becoming less and less common, may be seen. Butterflies are abundant, common, small and chalk-hill blues and marbled whites occurring frequently.

At Great Kimble there is another nature reserve. Here the rich flora includes adderstongue fern, blue fleabane, felwort and three orchids, bee, fragrant and pyramidal. In the deep coombs near Chequers is one of the finest natural boxwoods in England. The dense woods contain some rare mosses and provide shelter for foxes, badgers and the little muntjac deer which is fast spreading south from the Chilterns. Coombe Hill, owned by the National Trust, is 852 feet above sea level and affords splendid views over the clay vale and the Portland limestone outcrops on which Aylesbury and several villages have been built. Most of the hill is chalk but the soil on top is acid clay-with-flints, which accounts for the patches of heather, gorse and bracken which appreciate acid soils. Further east the path passes through Concord Wood where the Wildlife Trust protects the Chiltern gentian.

The last part of the walk takes us to the hills around Ivinghoe Beacon. At Pitstone Hill, fragrant orchids occur and also the rare field fleawort, which prefers the drier chalk slopes. Incombe Hole is an impressive coomb near Steps Hill which contains a badger's sett and is a favourite roosting place for migrant and wintering birds. You will no longer see the pasque flower which was once found here, partly because plants have been dug up in the past by unthinking visitors. No one who enjoys walking along the Ridgeway would now wish to damage the plant and animal life which naturalists are protecting for future generations.

Anyone living near the Ridgeway and interested in natural history or anyone making a study of the area would do well to consider joining the Berks, Bucks and Oxon Wildlife Trust, which maintains several reserves close to the Ridgeway.

5
Towns and villages near the Ridgeway
by Stuart Harrison

WILTSHIRE

Avebury

A lovely village with gabled Elizabethan manor-house, Saxon church, dovecote and a thatched great barn, Avebury is famous for its neolithic stone circle of about a hundred great sarsen stones. To reach the Ridgeway take the bridle road east to Overton Down, or the B4003 south-east to Overton Hill.

Bishopstone

This is a village of thatch and trees nestling in a hollow of the downs on the Oxfordshire border one mile north-east of the Ridgeway. The little stream flowing beside the interesting Norman church fills the village pond.

Chiseldon

Beloved by the writer Richard Jefferies, Chiseldon lies on the edge of the Marlborough Downs, south of Swindon. There are attractive thatched cottages opposite the little thirteenth-century church. To reach the Ridgeway, leave the village by A346 and after a quarter of a mile turn left (east) along a minor road (marked Ridgeway on the OS map) and rejoin the footpath after one and a half miles.

Marlborough

This market town has one of the widest main streets in the country. The sloping High Street contains some fine Georgian buildings and the back streets with their half-timbered cottages are worth exploring. The famous public school was built in 1843. For the Ridgeway, follow the A4 towards West Kennett for four and a half miles.

Ogbourne St George

The village is situated at one of the highest points of the Marlborough Downs. The manor stands on the site of an eleventh-century priory founded by Maud of Wallingford. The Ridgeway crosses the A346 just south of the village.

Swindon

A large industrial town offering excellent shopping facilities,

Cottages on the Ridgeway at Hallam, near Ogbourne St George.

Swindon is an important railway centre with a good train service. There is a new railway museum called 'Steam' illustrating the town's association with the Great Western Railway with exhibits from the age of Brunel and later. It is situated north of the Ridgeway: take A419, then A345 towards Ogbourne St George for about five miles.

Wanborough

Wanborough was once the key of Wessex, where three Roman roads met and two Saxon battles were fought. The parish church has a fourteenth-century stone spire with two rows of windows and a fifteenth-century pinnacled tower. It is one and a half miles north-east of the Ridgeway towards Liddington.

Winterbourne Bassett

This is a small village with village green and pub. Join the path on Hackpen Hill, crossing A4361, one and a half miles from the village.

OXFORDSHIRE

Ashbury

Near to the Wiltshire border, the village contains Elizabethan cottages, a Norman church, a fifteenth-century manor-house and a group of sarsen stones. To the east of the village is Wayland's Smithy. Take B4000 south-west of the church for one mile to the Ridgeway.

Aston Rowant

Trees and fine houses, both old and new, make this an attractive village. There is an interesting church and a broad village green. Travel south to the A40 and turn left to reach the Ridgeway after a quarter of a mile.

Benson

Lying back from the Thames, the village has a thirteenth-century church and some fine former coaching inns. For the Ridgeway, take the A4074 Reading road to the second roundabout.

Chinnor

On the eastern boundary of Oxfordshire, below the Chilterns, the church, with two fourteenth-century windows containing the original glass, has a picture gallery of thirteen brasses, nearly all from the fourteenth century. There are sixteen pictures of saints by Sir James Thornhill. Take B4445 into Chinnor, and where the main road turns right continue straight ahead for half a mile to the Ridgeway path.

East Hendred

This is another beautiful downland village, surrounded by orchards and fields, and with narrow lanes and colourful architecture to explore. For the Ridgeway, take the road south out of East Hendred for about two miles. After a right-angle bend turn right and continue for about half a mile.

Faringdon

This little market town has a good selection of shops and a bustling centre around an old pillared town hall. A mile south-west is a great tithe-barn. For the Ridgeway, take A420 south-west towards Shrivenham for about six miles. Turn left on to B4000 to Ashbury and continue for about one mile.

Goring

Twin town to Streatley on the Thames, Goring has an interesting range of shops and inns and facilities for boating. It is a leading tourist venue, with fine walks and views. The Ridgeway path passes through the town.

Kingston Lisle

This is a pretty village with an eighteenth-century manor and a church with Norman features. The famous 'blowing stone' on Blowingstone Hill is in the garden of a cottage south of the village. Take the main road through the village for one mile, crossing the B4507, to reach the Ridgeway.

Shrivenham

Shrivenham has a wide, tree-lined main street with a number of thatched cottages and shops. It is the home of the Royal College of Military Science. There are walks through woods and around the lake. For the Ridgeway, take B4000 south-east to Ashbury, then continue on B4000 for one mile.

Stanford in the Vale

A lively village in the Vale of the White Horse, Stanford has a late twelfth-century church, with a south porch built to celebrate the marriage of Anne Neville to Richard III.

Uffington

This village was the birthplace of Thomas Hughes, author of *Tom Brown's Schooldays* and *The Scouring of the White Horse*. There is a museum in the village.

Wallingford

This popular Thames-side town, with a fine long bridge, has the country's second oldest charter and defences built by King Alfred. It is a good centre for shopping and has several inns. There are riverside walks and facilities for boating. For the Ridgeway, cross the bridge, through Crowmarsh Gifford, to the A4074, turn right for Reading and go to the next roundabout.

Wantage

A busy market town surrounded by isolated racing villages, Wantage was the birthplace of King Alfred the Great, whose statue stands in the wide market place. It has an interesting local museum and is a good shopping centre. Take A338 through the town south for about two miles to the Ridgeway.

Watlington

At the foot of the Chiltern escarpment and Christmas Common, the narrow streets are lined by red-brick shops and cottages. The Watlington White Mark was cut into the hillside to the south in 1764. For the Ridgeway, take B480 south-east out of the town for one mile.

BERKSHIRE

Compton

Compton has old cottages, a fine village inn and an attractive church, on the edge of the village. Take the road north-east from Stocksmeadow Farm for about a mile and a half to reach the Ridgeway.

East and West Ilsley

These two villages in the heart of the downs are famous for their racing stables. East Ilsley has a saddler's shop three hundred years old and a village pond, while West Ilsley is tucked away in a wooded fold of the downs. For the Ridgeway, from West Ilsley travel one and a half miles north towards the A34.

Lambourn

An ideal centre from which to explore the downs, Lambourn has a twelfth-century church and sixteenth-century almshouses. The influence of the racing world is much in evidence. Take B4001 north for four and a half miles to the Ridgeway.

Streatley

At the foot of the downs in the Goring Gap, Streatley is a popular Thames-side resort. There are spectacular views. Join A417 and travel north for about one mile to the Ridgeway.

Yattendon

An immaculate village in wooded country in the south-east corner of the downs, Yattendon has the Manor House, the Grange, the church, the rectory, the Malt House and not least the charming Royal Oak inn as part of a perfect village scene. For the Ridgeway, travel two miles north-west towards Hampstead Norris, then take B4009 for about six miles to Streatley.

BUCKINGHAMSHIRE

Aylesbury

The centre of this county town is worth exploring with narrow Tudor alleyways and quiet paths around the church of Saint Mary. It is an important shopping centre. Take A413 for five miles south to Wendover, where the Ridgeway can be joined.

Ivinghoe

Near the Bedfordshire border, Ivinghoe Beacon, Pitstone windmill, a watermill, a fine church and a youth hostel make this unspoilt village a focal point for exploring.

Longwick-cum-Ilmer

Extending down from the Chilterns to the fertile Vale of Aylesbury and the Oxfordshire border, the parish also includes the charming little villages of Horsenden, Meadle, Owlswick, and a cluster of farming hamlets. From Longwick take A4129 towards Princes Risborough; the Ridgeway is just off A4010 south of the town.

The Market House in Princes Risborough.

Princes Risborough

Only a few miles from the Prime Minister's country residence at Chequers, the town is a busy shopping and commercial centre. There is some interesting architecture, including a brick market house with arcades and a wooden cupola. Join the Ridgeway path just off A4010 south of the town.

Wendover

Overlooked by Coombe Hill, this historic town contains many half-timbered cottages and red-brick houses and inns. The manor house and the fourteenth-century church are side by side down a picturesque lane. Cromwell and Robert Louis Stevenson stayed here, while Hampden, Canning and Burke represented Wendover in Parliament. Join the path near the Clock Tower Tourist Information Centre.

HERTFORDSHIRE

Aldbury

Set between the Ridgeway path and the woods and commons of the

Ashridge Estate to the east, Aldbury nestles around a village green, complete with duck pond, old stocks and a whipping post. Go north for two and a half miles to Ivinghoe and join the path at Ivinghoe Beacon.

Berkhamsted

The commercial life of this busy town centres on its long main street. There is a ruined castle, and the Grand Union Canal passes through the town. To join the Ridgeway, take A4251 towards Tring for three miles.

Tring

Another busy town close to the Ridgeway, Tring is a great attraction for naturalists. The Zoological Museum in Park Street has an unrivalled collection of mammals, birds and reptiles, while the Tring Reservoirs at the summit of the Grand Union Canal form an excellent nature reserve. Join the path at Tring station.

BEDFORDSHIRE

Dunstable

Dunstable Downs are famous for the spacious Whipsnade Wildlife Park and for gliding. Dunstable was once the home of a thriving straw-hat industry. The priory church dates from 1150 and was the scene of the trial of Katharine of Aragon. For the Ridgeway take B489 six miles to Ivinghoe Beacon.

6
Public transport

No one should be deterred from walking the Ridgeway because they do not wish to walk the whole length at one go, camping or seeking overnight accommodation, or cannot arrange to be met by car each evening. While public transport services are sparse in some areas of the route, especially west of the Thames, it is possible to walk the whole route in stages from a home base in London or other areas, using trains and buses to travel out in the morning and return in the evening. Indeed, walking the Ridgeway in this way makes an admirable project spread over a number of summer Saturdays (rather than Sundays, when most of the bus routes described below do not operate or are much less frequent).

Swindon is a good centre for buses in Wiltshire and is less than an hour from London (Paddington) by high-speed trains. By taking a bus from Swindon to Avebury, one could walk the Ridgeway to Ogbourne St George, from where there is a bus service back to Swindon. The second stage could end at the B4000, leaving the Ridgeway to walk down into Ashbury, which has buses to Swindon; as no regular bus routes cross the Ridgeway between Fox Hill and East Ilsley one would have to descend the hills to catch a bus at Wantage, which has regular buses to Didcot, linked by fast trains to Paddington. East Ilsley is served by the infrequent Newbury–Oxford route. Goring, whose station has frequent trains to London, Reading and Oxford, would be a convenient place to end or begin a day's walk. The bus service between Oxford and Henley via Wallingford stops on the A4130 near the Crown at Nuffield. Watlington has an hourly bus service to Oxford, and there is a less frequent service along the A40 (High Wycombe – Stokenchurch – Oxford), crossing the Ridgeway near Aston Rowant. Buses run from Chinnor to High Wycombe, Thame and Princes Risborough. Princes Risborough station has a frequent train service to High Wycombe and London (Marylebone) and also services to Aylesbury and Birmingham. Wendover is served by half-hourly trains from Aylesbury to Marylebone and Tring station by half-hourly trains from Euston to Milton Keynes. The bus service from Aylesbury to Luton, which has frequent trains to London (Thameslink line stations), runs through Tring and along the main road below Ivinghoe Beacon.

The services described here refer to Mondays to Saturdays. The publishers have endeavoured to ensure that the information was correct at the time of compilation, but all services, particularly rural bus routes, are liable to alteration or discontinuation and walkers are advised to contact the train and bus operators before travelling to establish actual times.

Bus companies operating around the Ridgeway include:

Arriva the Shires and Essex (Aston Rowant, Chinnor, Princes Risborough, Wendover, Tring, Ivinghoe): timetable enquiries, telephone 0870 608 2608.

Stagecoach in Oxford (Wantage, East Ilsley): information, telephone 01865 77 22 50.

Stagecoach Swindon & District (Ogbourne St George): telephone 01793 522243.

Thamesdown Transport (Avebury, Ashbury): telephone 01793 428428.

Thames Travel Buses (Wallingford, Goring, Nuffield, Watlington): telephone 01491 837988 or 874216.

For train times contact:
National Rail Enquiries; telephone 08457 484950.

The descent to Overton Hill.

Index